First Comes

LOVE

The Unmarried Guide to Finding Love

Larry A. Jackson
Breastplate Prayer Publications

First Comes Love

Breastplate Prayer Publications

Distributed by Frontliners Ministries
3715 Ridge Road
Charlotte, NC 28262

Cover Design: Tudor Maier
Editor: Valerie Hunt

Printed in the United States of America
ISBN: 978-0-9857687-6-8

Dedication Page

This book is dedicated to my five beautiful daughters, Latasha, Crystal, Charity, Courtney and Carmen who have dedicated their lives to pleasing the LORD and their parents. These are women of God and my wife and I are tremendously happy about where they are in life and believe that the best is yet to come.

Women of God thank you for making my stewardship over your lives easy!

Everything that I do happens because I married a woman who supports me completely and is beloved by all who meet her. Joanndra, I love you and pray to make the rest of your life better than anything we have already experienced.

The support system around me extends far beyond my family with a staff of people that are second to none; Annette Williams, Monique Johnson, Stephanie Briscoe, Autonette McLaughlin, Kinsza Virgil, Daphene Robinson, Joyce Pemberton and Apostle Diane Chappelle.

There too many spiritual daughters to name here but each of them knows how much they mean to my heart and it is with joy that I can have a father-daughter relationship with them.

My church family "Bethel Outreach International Church" is the kind of church that everyone should be a part of at least once in their life. Thanks for all that you do!

TABLE OF CONTENTS

Preface

There are many unmarried people today in and outside of the church who would like to find that special person and get married. One thing that I have always found interesting is the fact that most have never studied the subject.

Think about it for a moment, from the time you entered school how many times did you study marriage or how to make money? These two subjects will affect the lives of most people for a long time after they are out of school however very little to no instruction is dedicated to them.

Once we enter our chosen profession many companies will provide training to help us become more productive and efficient in our employment. Those who have had the pleasure and privilege of playing organized sports are given a play book associated with their sports teams that not only give instructions about the game and how to run different plays but also give information about the teams' code of conduct.

Instruction can be found throughout life connected with things we want and love to do and they are needed so that we can be successful. The problem I have found over the 30 plus years of working with people in ministry is that we think marriage is something we intuitively understand. It would also appear that the broader society believes the same since there is very little instruction presented about marriage during our formative years or even during our higher education years.

How you ever purchased a product that needed assembly and you just thought you knew how to put it together because it only had a few parts and it looked simple? The instruction sheet that includes pictures of all the parts is right in front of you but you just glance at it and throw it to the side. Once the product is put together a leftover bolt or a bracket is in the box or in your hand and you don't have a place to put it but it wouldn't be in the box if it wasn't necessary.

It seems to take too much time and afford to just read each step and perform the task as the instructions indicate and even though the product can possibly be used it is incomplete and not put together the way the designer intended.

It is the same way with marriage, seeing it from a distance and even watching your parents' marriage isn't enough since you aren't marrying your mother or father. Your mate will have different ideas about life and marriage and all that it involves and that means complete instructions will be needed with a step by step process so that no bolts or brackets are left out of the finish product. There are many people who have been in a lawyer's office or stood before a judge when facing divorce who clearly understood once they are there that marriage takes more than an inward knowing, it takes work.

This book and companion workbook is designed to start that work process in your life but should not be the only material used to understand marriage. The main book that should be used is the word of God (Bible) and it is always good to have a mentor that can help you apply the word of God to your life. I am so happy you are starting the process and using this book as your guide to finding love!

Introduction

Nursery rhymes are fun for children, designed to teach a life principle to young minds that can help them later in life. This teaching principle holds true for the nursery rhyme associated with the title of this book. Just in case you don't know the rhyme, here it is;

Jack and Jill sitting in the tree
K-i-s-s-i-n-g!
First comes love.
Then comes marriage.
Then comes baby in the baby carriage!

This rhyme is designed to place into the minds of children the principle of human relationship and the order of that relationship. Love is the foundation of the relationship and from that place marriage and children can then follow. This is not the first book written that uses the third line of this nursery rhyme as its title. There has even been a film that used the line as its title as well.

I do believe it could be the first book with this title that acknowledges the first love as a relationship between God and man as its foundation before a relationship between man and woman.

Since my book *The True Value of a Woman* was published, many unmarried women have asked me to help them understand how to prepare for marriage. These questions were posed even though there was an entire section of the book dedicated to the unmarried woman.

If you've read any of my other books, you know that I have five grown daughters who I dedicated this book to and you know that I've been married to the same woman for over 28 years. We have raised our daughters to understand the principles I wrote about in both True Value of a Woman books as well as in this book.

My wife and I prayed that our sons-in law would be men of God while the girls were still in grade school. One of our main prayers was that the girls would understand their value and live to set standards for others to follow.

It hasn't always been easy for the girls or even for us as parents to establish such a standard in a world where everything goes against that standard.

If you are a parent with growing daughters most likely you have had the "It's not fair!" discussion and if not it is on the way so just wait. The "It's not fair!" discussion surrounds what it appears young men can do or get away with that young women can't.

That the same teaching is received and the same bible is being read but there seems to be a double standard operating for young men and women in the church of Jesus Christ. We have had the "It's not fair!" discussion many times in our home related to what boys can do as opposed to girls. We made it through these years but it does mean that the discussion is over because they are grown sometimes there is a new level of talks that must take place.

Three of our daughters are still unmarried, and we continue to have conversations concerning their future and the standard they must set as adult women. These young women have their own jobs, cars, and ideas now, so the foundation established early in life was of great importance. As their father, it is my place to help them understand how to make sense of what they desire of their relationships.

Even though we didn't have any sons, I have mentored a number of young men in the same way it was mentioned in the dedication concerning my spiritual daughters and each one of these men are married and leading successful family lives. Several of their wives have thanked me for helping their husbands to become the men they married. Never did I make them think that there was one standard for them and another for my daughters. If anything was done in this regard I talked to them about establishing a greater standard so that their future wives would be secure in the marriage. Several of my spiritual sons would say **"It's Not Fair!"** that they were responsible for the love and had to carry all of the weight. But this is just the way Jesus taught us through the Apostles to understand the role of marriage for the man.

Bishop Wellington Boone did the same for me; he took an eager but unpolished young man and helped to make me the man many today respect and love. My wife has also thanked Bishop Boone for his involvement in my life. She also looked to Bishop early in our marriage to help me to make additional adjustments that could only be understood while we were facing them.

This book is written from the understanding of having been mentored, of mentoring others, and raising women to advance the kingdom of God in an hour where many violate divine standards, even in the church. If you read with an open mind, your life will increase greatly even before the Lord introduces you to your life mate!

Your First Love

Jesus revealed the secret to the proper view of marriage when the religious hypocrites tried to corner him with a "tough" question about who would be the husband of a woman, widowed seven times during her life, at the resurrection of the dead. Jesus said, "You're way off base, and here's why: One, you don't know your Bibles; two, you don't know how God works. After the dead are raised up, we're past the marriage business. As it is with angels now, all our ecstasies and intimacies then will be with God." *(Mark 12, The Message)*

Jesus identified our true and eternal marriage partner: God Himself. The Bible tells us that, as believers, we are both individually and corporately married to God. "For thy maker is thine husband; the Lord of hosts is His name, and thy redeemer the Holy One of Israel." *(Isaiah 54:5)*

Too many cultures view marriage as the pinnacle of existence -- the starting point where life really begins. The ideal spouse is an indispensable part of the "American Dream," and women especially are viewed as incomplete without a man at their side. The truth is that all of us can be complete with our true and eternal husband, God alone. Until the completeness He offers becomes a reality in our lives, marriage in the earth will only be a Band-Aid® on the gaping wound of emptiness.

Unfortunately, many unmarried Christians have bought into a worldly perspective of marriage. They have not allowed God to stir up their innermost passions and affections toward Him, and instead offer themselves all too readily to people they meet. When we resist our First Love, and bare the part of our hearts that is rightly His to someone who is not our spouse, we can also cause problems that must be managed in our future marriage before it begins. Our culture has lost the understanding of keeping ourselves, emotionally and physically, first for God, and then for the one whom He has chosen for us.

The more we really know God on an intimate level, as opposed to just knowing about Him on a mental level, the more we will find true satisfaction and fulfillment. Human marriage was created by God, and it is a wonderful experience when entered into God's way. Searching for a mate or accepting someone's advances because of increasing age, or feelings of loneliness, insecurity and boredom will not lead you into marriage God's way. Another thing you can be assured of God's way of marriage will never interfere with your First Love.

As was mentioned in the introduction "First Comes Love" is associated with a popular nursery rhyme but the bible used the first love phase to outline the church of Ephesus' relationship with the Lord. The church in Ephesus had many good works to their credit. *(Revelation 2:3)* They had persevered through trials, and demonstrated godly character. Despite this impressive track record, Jesus rebuked them for this: "Nevertheless, I have this against you, that you have left your First Love." *(Revelation 2:4)* All our efforts to live the good Christian life have little meaning if we lose our passion and fervor for the Lord Himself.

The call of God to unmarried Christians is clear: first we must return to our First Love. We must allow God to turn our hearts toward Him. Jesus told the Ephesian church to "Repent and do the first works..." and His command to those of us who have allowed our zeal to diminish is no different. When we return to Him as our true Husband, the precious mental and emotional energy that is wasted pursuing a fantasy life can be used to build the Kingdom.

This is the principle that is found throughout the bible and it was God's main focus after the fall to regain relationship with mankind (Man and Woman). Jesus came to restore everything that was lost because of the fall, even the broken relationship between the man and woman that was completely changed from the way it was designed in complete oneness to two separated individuals.

The scripture references below are just a small sample of the relationship the Godhead wants with humans and how the relationship between man and woman should be with each other and these two relationships look very much the same.

John 17:11 And now I am no more in the world, but these are in the world, and I come to thee. Holy Father, keep through thine own name those whom thou hast given me, that they may be one, as we are.

John 17:22 And the glory which thou gavest me I have given them; that they may be one, even as we are one:

Ephesians 5:31 For this cause shall a man leave his father and mother, and shall be joined unto his wife, and they two shall be one flesh.

Second, we must regain a biblical understanding of human relationships in general, and courtship and marriage specifically. Most unmarried Christians and singles that live a life outside of Christ have a confused vision of friendship and marriage that is made up of an unstable mixture of cultural pressures and a shallow understanding of the mind of God. When God renews our mind with His plan for all our relationships-- including marriage, we will be fulfilled in each season of our lives, and also we will understand better how to discern the will of God when it comes along.

The unmarried Christian is very concerned about the will of God for their lives and especially when their potential mate comes into the picture. When a person has their priorities right and they are developing and ministering to their First Love then the will of God is never an issue. God knows that they will not do anything to break their relationship with Him. The person clearly knows that He will only provide the best for their lives and will protect them against any and all things that could and would break their relationship.

Zechariah 8:2 Thus saith the LORD of hosts; I was jealous for Zion with great jealousy, and I was jealous for her with great fury.
Will you answer this call? Will you return to your First Love, Will you commit to make all your human relationships accurately represent the Kingdom of God to a dying generation? The stakes of these choices are very high. The world is longing to see unmarried Christians passionate for the things of God, unencumbered by the baggage of society. Then once married to show how God designed marriage from the beginning between a man and woman who love Him while functioning as one. Will you be the answer?

1. Love never gives lists
2. Love cares more for others than self.
3. doesn't want what it doesn't have.
4. doesn't strut
5. doesn't have a swelled head
6. doesn't force itself on others.
7. isn't always me first
8. doesn't fly off the handle.
9. doesn't keep score of the sins of other
10. doesn't revel when the others grovel
11. takes pleasure in the flowering of truth.
12. puts up with anything
13. trust God always
14. always looks for the best.
15. never looks back
16. keeps going til the end.

Making the Most of Your Unmarried Life

Our life on earth is made up of many seasons. Childhood, schooling, adulthood, unmarried life, employment, marriage, and parenthood are all examples of seasons of life, some of which overlap. Unmarried adult life is a season that may be practically non-existent for those who marry young, or last a lifetime for others. Some people are called to life-long unmarried status for the sake of the gospel, like the apostle Paul was. Others simply have a window of time between the point they reach adulthood and the time they marry. Whichever the case, being unmarried presents some remarkable opportunities to serve the Lord, serve other people, and expand your understanding of yourself and the world God has called you to impact.

Of course, some individuals find themselves unmarried after they lose their spouse to death, divorce, or abandonment. These situations are often accompanied by special needs, especially when there are young children to take care of. We will address this special category of unmarried people in great detail in Chapter 3. 1 Timothy 5:3-16 gives sound guidelines for how their needs are to be met. Their extended families and grown children are to first take the responsibility to see that they are cared for and loved; where these may be lacking, the church as a whole must meet the need. The circumstances of life don't change the standard of God and these people are held to the same standard of behavior as every other Christian: to conduct their selves above reproach.

SERVING THE LORD WITHOUT DISTRACTION

Paul spoke about his call to be unmarried his entire life, "For I wish that all men were even as I myself. But each one has his own gift from God, one in this manner and another in that. But I say to the unmarried and to the widows: It is good for them if they remain even as I am."
(*1 Corinthians 7:7-8 NKJV*)

Clearly, Paul knew that God does not call everyone to stay unmarried for life, but he saw something so awesome in his own unmarried life that he wished everyone else could take advantage of it, at least for the time it was given to them.

Being unmarried is a remarkable opportunity. It is so much more than "preparation for marriage," although certainly that can be part of it. God has given each of us our own gift, and until the season that He brings our life-mate into the picture, that gift is to know Him and enjoy being unmarried. If we fail to see being unmarried as the incredible blessing that it is, we will waste it. Not only will the Kingdom of God and our own character suffer with this waste, but we will be ill-prepared for marriage and parenthood. Perfect preparation for the next season God is opening up for us can always be entered into by fully embracing the season in which we find ourselves.

One of the key advantages of being unmarried and serving the Lord is that you don't have the obligations that accompany a spouse and children.

Once married, when will you have the opportunity to fast and pray like you do now? In most cases, you don't have to worry about preparing meals for your family, or earning money for college funds for your kids. You have more freedom to take a "prayer sabbatical" from your everyday life than you may ever have in the future. If you don't take advantage of that now, do you think you will ever do it when your obligations increase? Recently my wife talked with me about getting away to spend time alone with God. She asked me because once you are married, the Bible instructs that we don't have a right to set ourselves apart to God away from our spouse without their approval.

Another key advantage to an unmarried life is fewer distractions from God. Listen to Paul's beautiful exhortations to the unmarried: "I say this for your own profit, not that I may put a leash on you, but for what is proper, and that you may serve the Lord without distraction." (*1 Corinthians 7:3-5*

NKJV) As important as cleaning up after children and earning money for their education may be, they are at best "worldly" goals (only in the sense that they are temporary, not carnal) and they can distract. Any Christian husband or wife will tell you that family responsibilities can distract from consecration and devotion to God. A successful marriage is sustained by God, but takes major effort on the part of both spouses. Being pregnant (or having a pregnant wife), bearing children, and raising them requires time and energy that can move you away from seeking the face of God. How you utilize your unmarried life can become the launching pad to a great married life; if you are wasting your time now, it could establish habits that are difficult to change once married with added responsibilities becoming the seed bed for excuses not to pursue the Lord.

Of course when marriage and children are in God's plan, He gives grace for them.
However, before they come we should take advantage of the opportunity to be "single-minded," having our focus on God, and giving Him all our most intimate attention that will later be somewhat divided among family members. People who pursued God as hard as they could before they had a family of their own are the ones who continue to do so afterwards. If you are passive about your relationship with God now, how do you think it will be when you are immersed in other

obligations? My advice to unmarried Christians is to get grounded in living for the eternal now, when it is simpler. Live each day for the sake of expanding the Kingdom of God so that if you do find yourself one day up to your elbows in diapers and facing a mortgage, you will keep your eyes on Jesus and the responsibilities will be used to strengthen you instead of deter you from fulfilling your eternal destiny.

Above all, unmarried people must be content in their state. Despising unmarried life and yearning for marriage never made anyone a better husband or wife. Contentment comes from worshipping and being obedient to God, not from having all of your desires satisfied all the time. The opposite of contentment is covetousness, and God forbids that as one of the Ten Commandments. What this means is that God feels strongly enough about the sin of covetousness that He put it in the same category as adultery and murder.
1 Timothy 6:6 tells us that "...godliness with contentment is great gain," and Hebrews 13:5 exhorts us to "Let your conduct be without covetousness, and be content with such things as you have. For He Himself has said, 'I will never leave you nor forsake you.'" Being content in your current state affirms to God and the rest of the world, that He alone is more than enough to meet your needs.

SERVING OTHERS

As every Christian knows, an indispensable part of serving God is serving other people, "...especially those who are of the household of faith." (*Galatians 6:10*) This applies to the unmarried Christian even more for the reasons mentioned above, the relative lack of obligations and distractions. Why are married people frequently viewed as more stable servants in the church than young, committed, unmarried Christians? Although some of this may be an inaccurate perception, the rest is because of the unmarried person's inconsistencies.

Here is a question I have asked the unmarried people in my church: "Should a family with children who need to be fed and dressed beat you to church on Sunday?" It happens all of the time! In my mind the unmarried people in the church should be the ones primarily responsible for church operations and advancing the vision. The married people should feel like they are at a disadvantage because they lack the time to dedicate to the church's vision and advancement in the same way. Serving at church is one of the best ways a person can learn to serve other people as you serve the Lord.

Of course, you must be balanced. Over-committing yourself to too many activities will not glorify God, nor expand His Kingdom. If you happen to have a personality disposition to serve, you must be careful about over extending yourself. Remember that your time belongs to God, and you can't just give it away to everyone who asks simply to avoid disappointing someone or attempting to just stay busy.

The modern era has provided so many things that make life easy; providing our needs with very little effort on our part. Serving others can suffer when life comes to us so easy. Good service is hard to find even in places where service should be a premium. But this should never be said of those of us who are Christians since service has to do with love and the kingdom of God is built upon the foundation of love. However, many unmarried people need to be stretched in this area, especially if their parents did everything for them when they lived at home. Such people often believe that the world revolves around them and they consider their own interests before anyone else's. This is completely contrary to the nature of Jesus. (*Philippians 2:1-4*) Train yourself to always think of others first.

Some of the most effective ways to serve people is just by praying for them, talking to them, and opening your home to them for times of fellowship. As God moves, you may begin "exploratory" Bible study, even with non-believers, teaching them basic truths about biblical world-view. There are so many people who don't have true friends in their lives and you can become that person just because of your servant attitude.

WATCH AND LEARN

Being unmarried is also a unique opportunity to be an apprentice to someone who is married in order to learn the skills they have already acquired. Ideally, we should all learn this at home, but sometimes there are gaps in our knowledge. Are you an unmarried woman, unsure of how to serve your future husband, train your children in the fear and admonition of God, cook, and keep your home? Find a more mature woman with a godly spirit, a godly marriage, and children to serve. Ask to come into her home when it is convenient for her and learn how to clean, cook, watch children, etc., being open for instruction and correction in the way that you do things.

My wife used godly women in her life once we were married to instruct her but she also spent a great deal of time around her grandmother before marriage. After marriage my mother even played an important part in her life because of her willingness to learn and become the best wife possible.

Are you an unmarried man who is unsure of how to love your future wife, train your children, provide for and rule your home? Find a married man with a godly spirit, a godly marriage, and children. Maybe you can't come to work with him, but find ways you can help him, perhaps with yard work or running errands. In both cases, serve as you would want to be served in their position, and you will reap what you sow.

The Bible speaks of this principle and pattern, but many people look at this as old fashioned and can't see the benefit in connecting their lives to a more experienced person to learn what they know about living. Therefore, many of these people make mistakes in life that could have been avoided. Even with good parents and family structure it is always good to hear from someone else who can reinforce what they have taught you. Learning from your mistakes doesn't make you wise; learning from someone else's mistakes does!

EXPANDING YOURSELF AND YOUR WORLD

Our generation, for all the information available to us through various media, is frighteningly underexposed. Christians should be different. "Enlarge the place of your tent, and let them stretch out the curtains of your habitations. For you shall expand to the right and to the left, and your descendants will inherit the nations..." (*Isaiah 54:2-3*) God is God of the whole world. He loves the whole world, and He wants His people to understand how it works. Being unmarried is a crucial time to allow God to expose you to the "real world" through relationships with different kinds of people, as well as education and travel.

If you have the opportunity to go to college, seriously consider taking it. College is not essential to success in life, but it can be very beneficial. Obtaining skills for a career is actually the secondary purpose for higher education, not the first. Attending a good school will hopefully broaden your knowledge base, train you in the areas of critical and analytical thinking, and give you a challenging forum to preach biblical world-view. Don't bother if you are not going to work hard and be a radical witness for God's glory. Colleges are too full of lukewarm Christians who misrepresent God by compromising His standards, and whose grades are an embarrassment to Him.

If you have not yet been outside the country for a significant "overseas experience," pray and ask God to provide an opportunity for you to go on a short-term mission's trip, or an extended overseas visit. The goal is to obtain healthy exposure, not vacation. God can help you save or raise the money, if that is an issue; you really just need to have the vision for it. Until you have been outside of the comforts of your own culture, you have limited understanding of the world God is calling you to impact, and a single-sided perspective on yourself. Each time you go, you will find yourself expanded beyond what you could have imagined. You will also know if your relationship with God is a cultural phenomenon or a reality that transcends culture.

Do you see all of the advantages an unmarried person has over the married person, when they focus their attention on Christ and His Kingdom? Many unmarried people feel like they have the disadvantage because they don't have someone they can call husband or wife. With all of this attention on marriage, you would think once a person finally answered the call to marriage their relationship is worked on regularly and God is pursued even more, but that is not what happens. Many of these people get bored in the relationship and the pursuit of God is only a "church thing," but the passion that should be seen because two born again believers who love God have found each other isn't demonstrated. And it can be due to the fact they didn't learn to live their unmarried lives to the fullest.

Let Your Purpose Drive You!

Every Christian should be devoted to discovering and fulfilling the will of God for his or her life. This is what is known as a "purpose driven" life. It is divine purpose that motivates you to rise up with enthusiasm in the morning, and go to bed satisfied and tired at night. A purpose driven life is an understanding of eternity that gives meaning and energy to each activity, each interaction, and each task undertaken in a day. A purpose driven life is full of joy and short of complaints, full of hope and short of frustration, and full of peace and short of anxiety. This is different from the life of a non-Christian who is goal driven, because the Holy Spirit is the personification of our purpose, and the divine helper who guides us into its fullness. To better understand this principle, I recommend you read Bishop Wellington Boone's latest book, *Holy Ghost Is My Friend,* where he outlines what a relationship with Holy Ghost should really look like.

From the time we get saved to the time that we are called home to be with the Lord, we are meant to live this kind of life. We should have an inward sense of purpose in every season the Lord takes us through. Many unmarried people are eager to get married because they feel that marriage and children will give them a deeper sense of purpose.

However, a marriage is meant to be the product of two destinies that are already set in motion. Without a revelation of "team purpose," it is weak at best. Raising children without having your sense of purpose already established often leads to trying to live vicariously through your children, and placing your unfulfilled dreams on them.

For as long as we live, including our season of being unmarried, we must discover, embrace, and fulfill God's will for our lives. Every season of our lives involves simultaneously obeying God, bearing fruit for His glory, and preparing for the next stage. Seasons or stages are not the same as "levels" of knowing God. Marriage is not necessarily a promotion, although it does entail another level of responsibility; it is a season change. Marriage does not equal a badge of spiritual maturity; how you prepare for it will determine whether it takes you to another level in your devotion and consecration, as God intends, or whether it becomes a source of grief and stress.

Knowing God more passionately and intimately is a promotion. Responding to challenges righteously is a promotion. Successfully raising a disciple is a promotion. God releasing greater power and anointing to your words is a promotion. Sometimes your promotion may be acknowledged outwardly with an office in the church or on your job, but mostly it will not. Learn to hear approval and affirmation from God as your reward.

We will briefly address some aspects of leading a purpose driven life and fulfilling the will of God. Go after every spiritual promotion there is while you are unmarried. There is no need to wait to grow in God.

OCCUPATION VERSUS PURPOSE

Your job is not your purpose and your purpose is not your job, whether you are a minister or a janitor. Our culture confuses occupation with purpose, and thus in the Christian community we tend to use *career* and *calling* synonymously. Being a lawyer is part of a calling, not a calling in itself. Would Jesus' purpose and calling have been accurately described as: a carpenter, called to witness to other carpenters, and influence the system of carpentry in first century Israel? Do we remember Paul as a maker of tents who used his traveling as an opportunity to lead a few people to the Lord? Even though every one of us is called to be like Jesus, we tend to have a limited understanding of our purpose.

Your God-given purpose encompasses everything that you are, each relationship you have, and everything that you do. It involves who you are to your family and friends, as well your vocation and spiritual gifts. Thinking that your calling is limited to your job could cause you to miss the importance of being a friend to someone God has placed in your life. Too many people seem to view the vocational aspect of their calling as more important, more pressing, or more rewarding than the relationship aspect. These people too often end up failing God, their spouses, their children, and their friends.

Don't get confused by focusing on what job you will have as the definition of your purpose on this earth. Ask God to change your mind-set and to reveal to you how much greater His intentions are for you. You can actually be unsure of what to study in school or what job to take but still lead a purpose-driven life while you wait for God to speak to you. Proverbs 16:9 tells us "A man's heart plans his way, but the Lord directs his steps." Have a plan, and trust God to order your steps.

CHARACTER: THE REQUIRED COURSES

For the sake of illustration, let us compare the journey toward fulfilling the will of God with that of a medical doctor. There is significant time, energy, and money invested between the time a young ten year old dreams of being a surgeon, and the time she is operating on someone. As potential patients, none of us would have it any other way. Does God have a lower standard for bringing us into the fullness of our calling, whatever it may be?

First, the ten-year-old must complete elementary school, middle school, and high school. Then she must gain entrance to a good university, then medical school. After that, she must complete internship and residency and more training, depending on her specialty. Throughout college, she will take not only biology, but chemistry, physics, calculus, and English, none of which are directly related to what she will be doing when she is operating on a patient. These are known as "weed-out" courses, because people who can't survive them are not disciplined nor developed enough to practice medicine, even if the material they cover is not directly relevant to the profession.

Now, just because she spends all this time in school does not mean she must wait until she is a licensed physician to help treat people. In middle and high school, she can volunteer at the hospital; in college, she can travel in the summer with medical units to other countries. During medical school, she begins to fill crucial roles in the hospital. Once a doctor, she must continue to stay abreast of changing technology and new research to make sure she is giving her patients the best possible care.

Becoming Christ-like is to any Christian who wants to fulfill God's will what a college education is to anyone who wants to be a doctor. "Weed-out" courses like humility, patience, and self- control are required to go on; they are not just one semester classes, but life-long training. Too many Christians drop out at the elementary school level, or make it to college but fail these "weed-out" courses. Others make it through, but don't remain teachable, causing the ability and anointing they do have to become stale, just as a doctor's techniques become obsolete.

When we refuse the Lord's training, we are forced to pursue our dreams in our own fleshly strength, instead of flowing with His way. Too many people have built large ministries while holding unforgiveness, achieved business success while living in pride, or attained political office without learning to prefer others over themselves. *God has ordained all of us to have great influence in our generation, but the worst thing that can happen to us is that we would gain such influence without having the character to handle it.*

Following the Holy Spirit is an all or nothing deal. We cannot resist Him and get "into the flesh" in one area, and think we will be able to hear Him guiding us in another. We cannot ask Him to answer our new question if we won't listen to the last thing He told us, but this does not mean that we have to be perfect to do the perfect will of God. However, each time we resist the Holy Spirit building our character, our discernment gets cloudier, making it that much easier to resist Him the next time. All this affects our ability to perceive where He wants to lead us and to respond to Him obediently, leading to confusion. God is not the author of confusion; He wants His children to hear His voice clearly. A pure conscience and inward witness that God is approving us gives us confidence, even when we are unsure of certain decisions.

Many times, the types of decisions that we feel we need a direct word from God for are not terribly important to Him. God is far more concerned about the state of our hearts than the job we take or the city we choose. We want Him to give us signs and wonders about which apartment to rent, when He just wants us to learn to budget and choose wisely. We would like to see divine writing on the wall to know what to major in, when God would prefer we just work hard at whatever we pick.

VISION: DREAMS, DIRECTION, AND DETERMINATION

What are your dreams? What wild, fantastic, earth shaking exploits do you dream of doing for God and His Kingdom? As a follower of Jesus, saturated in the Word of God, your expectation should be sky-high for the things God wants to do through you. The dreams of someone who has tasted eternity make the American Dream of the spouse, job, money, house, cars and 2.5 children look like a death sentence of boredom. Dream big. Pray big. Write it all down and share it with your friends. But don't stop there.

Godly vision starts with such dreams, but goes a lot further. True visionary Christians don't just think about what they would like to do, but are devoted to the step by step process, day after day, of gaining character and making their dreams a reality. True, when we first get saved, many of our carnal dreams are put on the altar, but God places a burden in our hearts so much greater, that we are not satisfied until we see His Kingdom established in the earth. If this is not an accurate description of you, ask God to change you, and give you an internal picture of what His Kingdom is really like. Each revelation He gives you from His word brings the picture into greater clarity and focus. This is your sense of direction, the place where your purpose driven life is driving you.

Once you have direction for your life, it is much harder for the enemy to steer you off-course, or corrupt your purpose for living. It is essential that you write the pieces of your vision down *(Habakkuk 2:2)* as God gives them to you, keeping this sense of direction before you. Just like an unused muscle will atrophy and become lame, your heart's burden can become buried and die in extreme trials or the day-to-day grind of living.

Whatever your "job" for the moment, be determined to let God purify and work out His vision in you.

You must also pursue godly wisdom at all cost. *(Proverbs 4:6)* Wisdom will tell you how to accomplish your vision, because every opportunity or open door may not be from God. The fruit of godly wisdom is humility *(James 3:13, 17)*, so the wiser you become, the more humble you will become. The more humble you become, the more easily you can discern the difference between your own motivations and the will and voice of God. Put a premium on wisdom. Stay saturated in the Bible, in study, and in devotion. This is a simple spiritual discipline, not an option. Make sure you budget to buy tapes or books that can help you gain wisdom. Stay in contact with people who are wise, as demonstrated by their humility.

DO WHAT YOU KNOW TO DO

There is a saying that God can't steer a parked car. Inactivity is not a fruit of the Spirit, and the Bible mentions laziness and slothfulness far more often than other sins the church condemns. At the same time, activity doesn't equal productivity in the Kingdom. Some people keep themselves busy to avoid the Lord, or to generate an artificial sense of purpose. Still, as a purpose driven Christian, when the Lord hasn't given you a direct word, do what you know to do. Here are some common-sense guidelines for making decisions and fulfilling the will of God.

Pray. Sometimes the most important activity to pursue is prayer. This is often a cliché answer to problems, but don't knock it until you've really tried it. If Christians prayed half as much as they talked about how bad things are, there would be a prayer revival in the kingdom of God like never seen before.

Be Submitted In Your Heart; Seek Godly Counsel. In addition to asking God to reveal to you your own heart, seek the counsel of those who are your spiritual elders. These may be your own parents and other relatives and also those men and women of God who have been commissioned to leadership in the local church. Seek counsel in situations after you have prayed and are still unsure, or want to check your decision with a second opinion. Listen, and don't only go to people whom you think will tell you what is easiest to hear. Discipleship is a major key to spiritual growth, which is why the Lord told us to go make disciples. Making disciples is important, but He was telling disciples to go perform this task. It is important that you have a mentor in your life who can give the answer that no one else is willing to give. Do you have this person in your life? If not, it is important that you find someone to whom you give the right to deal with the things in you that are not Christ-like. Believe me, it will not feel good and you will want to change the agreement many times early in the process. Hang in there; it will get easier, and the benefits will be apparent.

Take Responsibility for Your Decisions. As an adult, you cannot look for others to make decisions for you. You will stand before God at the end of your life for what you have done with it, so you must embrace that responsibility here on the earth. A good leader will advise you and help you think through your decision, not control you.

"Whatever you do, do it with all of your heart, as to the Lord and not to men." (*Colossians 3:23)* Doing anything half-heartedly is not the will of God. Even if you are unsure of how long you are to be at a job or in a certain city, put your heart into it so you can gain everything you are supposed to gain while there. Work as unto the Lord and not to get paid or to gain approval from man. Live your life in every area in this fashion and stay in a repented state of mind if ever you fall short of this goal, and you will see the advancement of God in your life.

Don't Take Yourself Too Seriously. As mentioned earlier, decisions that we stress over are frequently not a big deal to God. He warns us that His ways are higher than ours *(Isaiah 55:8, 9),* and that we can only partially understand a fraction of His thoughts. We are often concerned about what will affect our day-to-day quality of living, while God is concerned about our eternal destiny.

So live with a heavenly focus, but enjoy life at the same time. I know people who will make an amusing statement and when those listening laugh, the person will cut off their laugh by saying something like, "I'm not joking." I was at a men's meeting and one of the men shared a very funny story; when the group standing around started to laugh, he cut us off with the statement, "No, I am serious!" Everyone stopped laughing, but the awkward silence we experienced wasn't fun at all.

The gentlemen could have accomplished the same thing by allowing the laughter and even joining with it before advancing the story. We could have understood the seriousness and still enjoyed the story. Sometimes people are so tight that it is difficult for them to enjoy life and just have fun. I believe Jesus was full of joy and had fun all of the time with the disciples, since it is clear that He was full of the Holy Ghost.

For the kingdom of God is not meat and drink; but righteousness, and peace, and joy in the Holy Ghost. (*Romans 14:17*) Jesus was the demonstration of the Kingdom of God in every way, so we should allow people to see the Kingdom through our right standing with God, peaceful living with others, the joy expressed in every area of life, and being filled with-- and led by-- the Holy Ghost.

Your Growing Relationship with Your Parents

The Kingdom of God is a web of relationships, orchestrated and sustained by God. Every believer is joined personally to God, and then connected at the heart to family members and friends. When Jesus was questioned about the most important commandment, He said, "You shall love the Lord your God with all your heart with all your soul, with all your mind. This is the first and greatest commandment. And the second is like it: You shall love your neighbor as yourself.' On these two commandments hang all the Law and the Prophets." (*Matthew 22:37-40*) *The quality of our relationship with God is demonstrated in the quality of our relationships with other people.*

Being unmarried is the best and easiest time to get our relationships with people right. Having a spouse and children of your own is a tremendous responsibility before God, and *the best preparation for being a godly spouse and parent is to be a godly son or daughter, and a godly friend.* The transition from childhood to adulthood will bring additional changes to your relationships with your family and friends. These changes can be stressful, but they don't have to be.

The family was first created by God when He brought Adam his wife, before the church, government, or any other institution in the earth. God chose the family as the primary building block of society, just as cells are the building block of the human body. The family in America has been in decay for decades now. Part of the redemptive plan of God for mankind is to "...turn the hearts of the fathers to the children and the hearts of the children to their fathers..." (*Malachi 4:6*)

Whether your parents were perfect Christians or caused you tremendous pain, God wants you to understand the way He designed family and wants each of us to become totally invested in the process. It is through parenting that the family structure is advanced, and while it is clear that some parents have been very poor examples of God's love, others have done an excellent job raising their children.

God wants you to obtain every good quality your parents have and to build on them. Where they have weaknesses, He wants to perfect you and use you redemptively. Remember that when God allows you to see weaknesses in your parents, the first person He wants to change is you. People who refuse to inspect their own lives miss and many times reject this principle. The standard comment is, "There is nothing wrong with me, it is them and how they act." I have experienced people attacking issues in others that can be found with very little effort in their own lives. Jesus told us to always pull the beam out of our own eye before trying to remove the speck in someone else's eye. Follow this pattern even when you don't think there is a beam, and you will not live life gripped by pride.

LIVING THE COMMANDMENT

The Bible tells us clearly that children are to "Obey [their] parents in the Lord." (*Ephesians 6:1*) This obedience holds for all things (*Colossians 3:1*), unless of course, a parent is telling his child to sin. God set this up as part of the order of the family, not to enable parents to dominate or lord it over their children. Parents are to demonstrate the nature of God as a Father to their children and train them to be like Jesus (*Proverbs 22:6*). God takes it very seriously when they fail to do this. Jesus said, "But whoever causes one of these little ones who believe in me to sin, it would be better for him if a millstone were hung around his neck and he were drowned in the depth of the sea." (*Matthew 18:6*)

One of the Ten Commandments given by God to Israel was to "Honor your father and mother that your days may be long upon the land which the Lord your God is giving to you." (*Exodus 20:12*) This commandment was given to people of all ages, not just to children. *Children* are *required to **obey** and *honor their parents; adults are simply required to honor them.*

The American Heritage Dictionary defines an adult as "One who has attained maturity or legal age." Exactly when a child becomes an adult varies somewhat from culture to culture, but two important elements are spiritual maturity and financial independence. Before God, parents still remain the spiritual covering for their adult children until they are married (*Genesis 2:24*). While God no longer requires adults to obey their parents, they should allow their lives to be open and vulnerable before them, asking their advice and listening to their godly counsel. Secure parents, like God, will not feel the need to dictate every aspect of their children's lives, but instead will delight to see them learning to make righteous decisions on their own.

Needless to say, this environment does not necessarily exist within every American family, whether it is Christian or not. We will briefly address three realistic scenarios; many experiences will fall somewhere in between the three:

"My parents (or unmarried parent) aren't saved, but we get along really well." Of course God wants your parents to be saved, and there will be some limitations on the advice and counsel they are able to give you because they do not have a relationship with God. Make sure you have spiritual covering at your church and that there is someone to give you balanced counsel from a sound biblical perspective. Nonetheless, God knew they would be your parents and has given them wisdom for you. Acknowledge their place in your life and keep them informed of your decisions, so that they may see the Lord guiding you and they feel embraced by you. Showing them love and appreciation may be the best witness you can give. Of course you should never be hindered in sharing the Gospel and the Word of God with them as He opens doors to do so.

"My parents (or unmarried parent) aren't saved, and we don't get along well." Above all, you must remember that God is sovereign. He would not have given you to your parents if He didn't have a plan for your life. Even though your parents didn't fulfill their responsibility to you He has a plan to heal you of all your wounds and reveal Himself to you in the midst of all of the challenges. If you are holding anger, bitterness, or unforgiveness in your heart, it is critical that you seek the Lord to help you release it. Other areas of your life will not be right unless you are at least attempting to get past such hurts. Talking to someone without being self-indulgently introspective can really help, but many times there are no easy answers and God simply has to visit you.

If you live at home, make sure that laziness or disrespect never mars your witness. Your parents should never have to get on your case about cleaning your room, helping with household responsibilities, or being out too late, etc. If there is anything you need to repent for to your parents, do it as soon as possible. If doing this in person or over the phone is too hard, try starting with a letter. You may feel as though the situation is 95% their fault and only 5% yours, but you must repent for your part anyway. Romans 12:17-21 makes it clear that we must do everything that we can to live at peace with all men. Make sure that before God you are doing all you can without compromising biblical principles. Once you are secure in your conscience, trust the Lord to do the rest. Trust Him to heal you completely from all of the pain of your past; it may be a process which takes several years, but He will be faithful to complete it.

Make sure you have covering and encouragement from your church. You will notice I keep coming back to this point, but it is very important in your spiritual growth. If your parents are abusing you or putting you in any physical danger, seek counsel from your pastor, and make sure that you are always in contact with someone who can help you.

"My parents are saved, but we have trouble seeing eye to eye." In some ways, this is the most awkward situation. As with non-believing parents, make sure that there is nothing on your end that needs to change for the relationship to improve. Know that it is God's will for there to be unity in your family, and that He is willing to move powerfully to make that happen. Do your very best to be respectful and to live above reproach.

Remember that as parents, they have extremely strong emotions toward you that you will be unable to fully understand until you are a parent yourself. Sometimes they may respond to you out of these emotions in a way that seems irrational. Be patient with them. Try not to interact with them when you are "in the flesh." "The beginning of strife is like a dam breaking; Therefore stop contention before a quarrel starts." (*Proverbs 17:14*) The point you are making may be right, but it's irrelevant if your spirit isn't right.

As we mentioned earlier, remember that God reveals weaknesses in your parents to you so that He can change you, not so that you can criticize them. Criticizing and complaining will not bring deliverance; it will only spread the problem. No matter how much we swear we will never do certain things the way our parents did, we are actually doomed to repeat their mistakes or overcompensate for them if we are not healed from them God's way.

POWER STRUGGLES

Power struggles between parents and children can start a few months after birth and continue into adulthood. They are frequently rooted in parents' desires to control their child instead of training and leading him, or caused by their inability to respond wisely to the child's rebellious behavior. Hopefully, when you become a parent, or if you are currently raising a child or children yourself, you will be wise enough to avoid too many power struggles with them. The first step in this is to be mature enough not to have a defiant attitude toward your parents. You can respectfully disagree with them without being rebellious in your heart. Remember that you will reap what you sow. Do you want your children (or even disciples the Lord sends to you) to treat you the way you treat your parents?

Choose your battles wisely. Don't argue about stuff that doesn't matter. Don't argue when you know you are wrong, such as when you've failed to keep the areas you are responsible for while at home in order. If you live on your own, remember parents are always watching to see if you are handling your life in a responsible manner. It is always easy to say that you are now grown and living on your own and it is not their business how you live and handle your money or your children. Just keep in mind that God isn't viewing your relationship with your parents the way you are and that we should always live to please Him. Work very hard to keep the peace and harmony when dealing with parents and family.

Save the disagreements for things that are really important to you, and make sure that to the best of your knowledge, it is the Lord leading you in that decision. Don't play emotional games, especially when you no longer live at home. Don't be deceptive or manipulative in any way. Be straightforward and honest, and pray for lots of wisdom. Consider Jesus' example in Luke 2:41-52. Jesus, at age twelve, was at the age of accountability according to Jewish custom, but still in His parents' care. He had an honest confrontation with his parents without being rebellious.

VISION FOR YOUR FUTURE

Ideally, parents should take on a supportive or coaching role with their children in the teen years. Having already trained them in righteous behavior, parents now help their children think and pray through the growing number of decisions they are learning to make on their own. Unfortunately, much conflict between young adults and their parents surrounds the vision for their future. Choosing a college, a major, and a career can stir up a lot of tension when your parents have different opinions and expectations for you than you have for yourself.

Sometimes, as mentioned earlier, parents are trying to live vicariously through their children, wanting them to fulfill their own unfulfilled dreams. On the other hand, some parents take little or no interest in what their children find pleasure or interest in. So if your parents have an opinion about what you are doing, make sure you hear them all the way out. Let them know you are listening to and praying about their advice.

The above statement only holds true to the degree that your parents' dreams for you agree with God's plans. You will have to answer to God at the end of your life for what He has called you to do, not what your parents expect. Consider the example of Zacharias, the father of John the Baptist, in Luke 1. Zacharias and Elizabeth were righteous before God (v. 5) and yet God had to supernaturally shut Zacharias' mouth to reveal to him his son's destiny. John the Baptist would have normally become a priest like his father, and was going to be named after his father (vv. 59-64), but God had other, somewhat unconventional plans for him. If you are having conflicts with your parents about similar things, believe God to reveal Himself to them as He did to Zacharias and Elizabeth.

In some cultures, children can be in bondage to their parents' dreams. Particularly if your parents made great sacrifices to pay for your education and/or bring you to this country, you may feel you owe it to them to do exactly what they want, even when you are an adult. In these cases, remember that loyalty to God must come before loyalty to parents, and that this is frequently a test of discipleship (see *Luke 14:26*). Remember the man who wanted to bury his father before he would follow Jesus (*Matthew 8:21-22*)? He missed his chance to become a disciple because he yielded to family pressure and tradition.

GENERATIONAL SINS/CURSES

Conventional wisdom tells us that the compromises of one generation become the vices of the next. Statistics have shown that couples who "sleep around" before getting married may find their children having children out of wedlock. Couples who speak against their pastor in front of their children may find their children refusing to attend church when they become older.

God wants to bring the opposite trend to pass in your life. He wants the weaknesses of the generation before you to become your greatest strengths, in which you not only flourish personally, but pass on to your children. Whatever trends God reveals to you, believe that He will not just suppress the behavior in your life, but completely obliterate it from your lineage.

Covenant Friendships

God created us for fellowship with Him and with our fellow man. When our relationship with Him and/or with those He has placed in our lives is not flourishing, it becomes tempting to seek comfort, security, and fulfillment outside of the will of God. Some isolate themselves and are consumed in their work, or other activities. Others get involved in inordinate relationships, which is any relationship that violates biblical guidelines and does not glorify God.

Friendships, whether among blood siblings or the family of God, are found throughout the Bible, and are a very important part of life as God intended it. God has called us to be committed to people He places in our lives in order to accomplish His will. Proverbs 13:20 tells us, "He who walks with wise men will be wise, but the companion of fools will be destroyed." *The type of friend you are and the types of friends you choose reflect the depth and quality of your relationship with God.*

WHAT KIND OF FRIEND ARE YOU?

Because we are all basically selfish by nature, we tend to be far more concerned with how others treat us, as opposed to what kind of character qualities we demonstrate to other people. Drawing from 1 Corinthians 13, which tells us the qualities of love (See Proverbs 17:17) and Galatians 5:22-24, which tells us the fruit of the Spirit, evaluate yourself to see if you are the kind of friend Jesus is:

Are you a *good* friend? Sounds simple enough. Would you want to have someone like yourself as a friend? Do you treat other people the way you would like to be treated?

Are you a *patient* friend? Are you willing to go through difficult times with someone, or do you become easily frustrated?

Are you a *kind* friend? Do you do and say everything with a person's best interest at heart? Do you excuse yourself from hurting someone's feelings because of your own emotions or mood?

Are you a *humble* friend? Do you need to be the center of attention all the time? Do you try to dominate every conversation you are in? Do you listen attentively to other people, even if they are not "important?"

Are you *a faithful* friend? Are you loyal to the people close to you, or do you simply attach yourself to whoever is around? Do you defend your friends to someone who speaks against them, or do you go along with anyone's opinion? Can your friends count on you to keep your word to them? Do you make sacrifices for other people, even when they have nothing to give you back?

Are you a *non-envious* friend, for lack of a better word? Are you just as happy to see your friend succeed or get blessed as you are to experience it yourself? Would you rather see your friends honored than be honored yourself? Would you pass up your own opportunity to get ahead to see your friend succeed?

Are you a friend who *rejoices in the truth?* Are you willing to share the truth in love for someone's good, even if it means risking offense or conflict?

WHAT KINDS OF FRIENDS DO YOU CHOOSE?

This is also a very important question. Proverbs 12:26 says, "The righteous should choose his friends carefully, for the way of the wicked leads them astray." Unless you place yourself around people who are more mature or more consecrated than you, you have a greater chance of backsliding in your commitment to the Lord.

Of course you are also called to be the salt and light of the earth. You should have friendships with non-believers as well; your life should show them how they need to live. However, *non-believers cannot meet your fellowship needs,* and you should always be sure that when you are with them that you are the one doing the influencing, not the other way around.

There are three types of friendships that you should seek God to have at each stage of your life: someone overseeing you, someone walking with you in covenant, and someone you are pouring your life into. This principle is spelled out in the book *True Value of a Woman*, concerning Naomi and Ruth's relationship and friendship that was the pathway to Jesus' lineage.

If you look at your life and find it lacking one or more of these relationships, ask the Lord to provide them and the people will soon manifest. Some of these people can be found in your family, church, and even in your profession, so it is very important that you open your eyes and heart to their involvement in your life. Pray for a willing heart to accept His provision, whatever the package. Are you willing to make friends outside of your race or social class? Are you willing to be mentored by someone younger than you? Are you willing to disciple and serve someone whose personality gets on your nerves? Answering these questions before the situation presents itself will help you to avoid conflict later.

RECEIVING FROM SOMEONE

Depending on your circumstances, this could be a peer mentor, an older Christian, or a pastor or elder in your church. It is amazing how many Christians feel completely qualified to tell other people what to do when they don't answer to anyone themselves. Who can vouch for your life before God? Who can tell you, "No?" Who can correct you when you are wrong? Everyone has blind spots in their discernment, so it is crucial to have someone like this in your life. Note: *peer mentorship is not a substitute for pastoral covering.* Every Christian who leads others must do so in harmony with the God-given institution of the local church.

Another important thing to remember is that although *you can learn from anyone, you don't want everyone's spirit.* Be teachable, not just in your youth, but for the rest of your life. However, if being a young person makes you a target for needy, would-be "disciple-ers," use wisdom. Be polite, but don't put yourself in a situation where someone is acting out their unwanted leadership instincts on you all the time. Look for someone whose life before God you want to imitate, not just the most aggressive person out there. Remember that the ultimate standard is the Word of God, so whatever you are receiving must thoroughly agree with the Bible.

For obvious reasons, it is ideal for the mentorship relationship to be between members of the same gender. Don't deliberately search for members of the opposite gender to disciple you. Always conduct yourself above reproach, giving no room for the enemy to even bring accusation. Too many inordinate relationships start out under the guise of "mentorship," or praying together, so be careful.

HAVING SOMEONE WITH YOU

Living for God is an awesome adventure, and there are people with whom He has called you to enjoy the excitement and challenges. Proverbs 18:1 reminds us that "A man who isolates himself seeks his own desire; He rages against all wise judgment." Real friends keep us real. They not only help us get through our challenges, they prevent us from taking them too seriously. After a point, being by yourself in a challenge can magnify it out of proportion. If you are an introvert and find it more comfortable to be alone a lot, be careful that you are not isolating yourself. At the same time, if you are an extrovert, make sure that you do not allow yourself to become peer-dependent (on affirmation from peers rather than God.)

Because they are people, friends will disappoint you. Nevertheless, friendship in the Bible is a covenant term, not dissimilar from the commitment associated with marriage. Do you have friends who value you for who you are, whom you can count on through tough times and easy times? If so, do not neglect those friendships; they are a gift from God. If not, ask God to send you someone.

Just because you are not in a mentorship relationship with your friends doesn't mean that God doesn't have a lot to teach you through them. Everyone has different experiences in life and with God. As a Christian, you should have friends from all different cultures and classes. Their perspectives will show you aspects of the Kingdom of God to which you would have otherwise been blind. Beyond all this, as an unmarried Christian, have fun with your friends. Plan vacations, road trips, mission trips and all the other activities that will most likely be more difficult to find time for later in life.

HAVING SOMEONE RECEIVE FROM YOU

Volumes could be written on the importance of discipleship, but without being too wordy, here are some important questions to keep in mind as God sends people to you to lead.

Can God promote your spirit?

It is not just what you know, but who you are that will be reproduced in those you lead. You can teach about prayer all day, but if you don't have a life of prayer, your words are of little value. Be open and vulnerable with those you lead; don't set yourself up as some perfect person you're not, because you will be found out eventually.

Are you willing to out-serve those you lead?

Most Christians think that mentoring someone is just preaching to them, but Jesus' words and example tell us that you will never lead someone God's way unless you out-serve them. Are you telling them how to be a Christian, or are you showing them?

Are you leading people to be greater than yourself?

The goal of pouring your life into someone is to see them do greater works in the Kingdom than you. They should not just follow in your footsteps, but exceed you. Too many would-be mentors need to be needed. They find it threatening when someone who used to look up to them becomes more self-sufficient or ceases to need them in the same way. Many times, they will respond by becoming hyper-sensitive to that person's remaining weaknesses, or claiming that they are "not ready" for this or that.

Jesus told His disciples that they were ordained to do even greater works in the Kingdom of God than He had done (*John 14:12*), and He was committed to taking them to the place where that would become a reality. It is also important not to go to the opposite extreme of pretending that people are somewhere where they aren't. Use wisdom, and always remember that, while someone may be entrusted to you to care for, he or she ultimately belongs to God.

Are you submitted to someone? This point has already been made, but cannot be overemphasized. *If you are not leading a submitted life, you have no business trying to lead others.* You have blind spots and you will lead people astray if you don't have anyone checking them. Fear God.

A WORD ON COMMUNICATION

Good communication skills are a product of knowing the ways of God, not studying psychology. God is the expert communicator, always speaking out of the right motivation, with the perfect combination of truth and love. Being a good listener, as well as knowing when to speak and when to keep your mouth shut is extremely helpful in every relationship. If you master good communication habits in friendships, it will make your transition to marriage that much smoother.

James 1:19 exhorts us to "Let every man be quick to listen, slow to speak, slow to wrath." Obeying these simple instructions can make all the difference in what kind of friend you are, as well as what kind of spouse you will be. *Listening is not just keeping quiet while someone else speaks; it is giving attention to their words.* God is an attentive listener who hears our prayers, even though we are completely insignificant when compared to His greatness. He has plenty of important things to say, but He still takes time to listen. Willingness to listen to someone should never be dependent on their stature as someone important. Listening well to others is a demonstration of how well you listen to God.

A good listener processes the information heard in order to respond appropriately to what has been said, asking questions when necessary. These questions are asked in order to clarify the listener's understanding, not challenge one's credibility. This type of listening requires that the listener be secure enough not to try to defend himself, even when the speaker is venting about something. A real listener is more concerned about accurately understanding what has been said, than pleading his or her own cause.

Good communication requires not only good listening, but wise speaking. The book of Proverbs is full of excellent instruction on the use of our words. The keys to speaking wisely are truth, pure motivation, and discretion. Everything we speak to one another must be true and motivated, out of love, to edify the hearer.

But speaking the truth in love, may grow up into him in all things, which is the head, even Christ: (*Ephesians 4:15*)

Possessing discretion, and knowing the appropriate time and manner to say something is just as important. Many times in Scripture this understanding is directed at women but men need to learn the principle as well.

Proverbs 11:22 says, "As a ring of gold in a swine's snout, so is a lovely woman who lacks discretion."

There are many excellent and exhaustive books you can read to help you improve your communication skills without compromising the truth. This is an area that must be studied continually and adjusted throughout a lifetime. Take time after every encounter, and especially disagreements, to determine how you could have communicated differently or better for the next time the opportunity presents itself. Always be ready to repent when the Holy Spirit illuminates places where there are blind spots keeping others from understanding or receiving your communication.

It is the responsibility of the speaker to secure that the hearer understands what is being said, and not the other way around.

Let your speech be always with grace, seasoned with salt, that ye may know how ye ought to answer every man. (*Colossians 4:6*)

But he that prophesieth speaketh unto men to edification, and exhortation, and comfort. (*1 Corinthians 14:3*)

Changing that in the hearts and minds of people would cause a major shift to take place across the landscape of not only the church but the entire generation. But let this start with us and see how far it can be advanced in the lives of those people near and dear to our hearts.

All of the things in this chapter will help to make true friends and the Bible tells us that if we show ourselves friendly, friends will be the result of that action. Treat people like you want to be treated and reap the benefits.

Living Above Reproach

Male-female relationships are a sensitive topic, to say the least. There are many different philosophies regarding proper conduct between men and women, reflecting many different worldviews. Closely tied to them are various views of sex, ranging from the complete acceptance of uncommitted sex, to the demonization of all sex, even within wedlock. God did create men, women, marriage, and sex, and left us quite adequate instructions on how He feels about all of these issues. *Our goal, as Christians, is not to create an unrealistic legal standard to adhere to but instead to rise up to* the *standard God has had for His people all along.*

Proper conduct among unmarried Christians not related by marriage or blood is quite simple: they are brothers and sisters. The vast majority of the time, this should be a very easy principle to follow. Most distractions and difficulties occur when people are not finding enough satisfaction and purpose in living for God, or are overly concerned with getting married and begin to view everyone as a potential mate.

Tragedy often ensues when Christians embrace a worldly view of male-female relationships and the standards that govern them, ignoring the biblical perspective. Often they cry that "The Bible doesn't say you can't kiss," or "The Bible doesn't say you can't have a boyfriend," without bothering to read and pray to see what the Bible does say. Let's take apart a few of the myths about dating and sex that are fashionable views in our generation:

MYTHS ABOUT DATING

1. Dating is an acceptable goal in itself.

For the sake of discussion, we will define the type of dating we are talking about as spending time alone with someone for whom there is romantic interest. These days, it is considered acceptable for young people to have "boyfriends," or "girlfriends" even if they are far too young and immature to be considering marriage. No matter what the norm in society may be in any given era, the Bible's standard does not change.

If you read through the Bible, you will notice that God describes and gives guidelines for many different types of relationships. Regarding romantic relationships between men and women, God recognizes only betrothal (such as Mary and Joseph) and marriage (such as Abraham and Sarah) as legitimate. All other types of male-female romantic relations were termed fornication, adultery, or incest. You cannot find anything in the Bible that sanctions having a boyfriend or girlfriend without working toward the goal of marriage.

Does God approve of such a relationship, but neglect to recognize it in the Bible and give instructions for appropriate behavior? Proper conduct in relationships is not something the Bible leaves up to cultural interpretation. All husbands must love their wives as Christ loved the church, regardless of where they grew up. Likewise, all who desire to please God must follow His word for their conduct regarding the opposite sex.

2. Having multiple dating relationships is a valuable way to learn about relationships before getting married.

It is very true that you can learn a lot from dating a lot of different people. You will learn about yourself, and about how you relate intimately to someone who is not your husband or wife. God is faithful to redeem our sinful experiences when we repent of them, using them as testimonies to others and teaching us valuable lessons. However, that is never a reason to try to get into such a situation. Everything valuable you could possibly learn by dating the wrong person (i.e., the person you don't marry), God can teach you better, if you allow Him. No committed, repentant, Christian who has dated others before marrying will ever advise you to do what they did.

Dating others before getting married is an avoidable mistake! God did not ordain you to bond with and break off from ten people before becoming one with your spouse. (By the way, emotional bonding is just as significant, and often leads to physical bonding). He ordained you to keep yourself for the right one in the right time!

(Disclaimer: Not all betrothals end in marriage. However, it is far less damaging to part from someone when the relationship was overseen by parents or pastors, and where there was lots of prayer and no physical contact, than it is to part from a boyfriend or girlfriend. Easy break-ups are found far more often on television than in real life.)

3. <u>Dating a lot before marriage is healthy and normal</u>.

This myth goes hand in hand with the first two. Many young, Christian women find that their parents became upset and worried when they informed them that they did not want to date until they were ready to marry. Likewise, even more parents worry that their sons are homosexuals when they make similar commitments. Our parents' and other older people's views on dating vary a lot from culture to culture, and generation to generation. There are still many who think that having a boyfriend or girlfriend is not only acceptable, but desirable! They may not have a clear grasp of the Bible's teaching, or they may not have had a good testimony themselves as unmarried and don't know how to deal with your stand for righteousness. Ask God to give you wisdom in dealing with them humbly, but without compromising.

A wise man will hear, and will increase learning; and a man of understanding shall attain unto wise counsels: (*Proverbs 1:5*)

For by wise counsel thou shalt make thy war: and in multitude of counsellors there is safety. (*Proverbs 24:6*)

Committed Christians should be social people (not just social *media* people) in the best sense of the word. However, we cannot be deceived into the world's lie that having multiple romantic (emotional or physical) relationships with the opposite sex is a healthy way to fellowship. A quick word about "evangelical dating" (thinking that you will lead someone of the opposite sex to the Lord by spending extensive time with them): DON'T. There is never an excuse for compromising the standard of God by spending inappropriate amounts of time with a member of the opposite gender, no matter how needy he or she is. If you violate this principle, your little convert, assuming he or she does get saved, will likely end up even more lukewarm than you.

Be ye not unequally yoked together with unbelievers: for what fellowship hath righteousness with unrighteousness? And what communion hath light with darkness? (*2 Corinthians 6:14*)

We are called to evangelize the lost, which means being in the company of those who don't know our Lord and His saving grace. It doesn't mean we are to have intimate relationships with those people in an attempt to win them to Him. Your focus and purpose will become cloudy because of a heart that will protect the person and dismiss their lack of commitment to your Savior.

4. Dating is the only (or the most) fulfilling way to have companionship.

As we have mentioned, human beings were created with the need for companionship with our fellow man, which comes from God. Many young people fall into ungodly or untimely relationships out of this desire and need for companionship. The devil deceives us to think that life is boring and lonely without romantic involvement with the opposite sex. The picture he wants to paint in our minds is that going out with friends is okay, but a date is exciting. Having friends that like you is okay, but what you really need is a boyfriend who really "loves" you. Given how shallow most Christians and thus most friendships are, it is easy to see why people fall into this psychological trap.

God knows what we need, and His perfect will encompasses what is best for us. God has ordained the need for human companionship to be met in the family and in the church, with the covenant relationships discussed in the previous section. True covenant friendships with purpose make pointless dating look repulsive!

When you have a circle of peers that are going for God with you, there is no limit to the adventures that await you. Even if you don't know any serious Christians now who will be committed to you, start praying. God has not forgotten what you need and He will surely honor your desire to have godly fellowship and companionship.

MYTHS ABOUT SEX

1. <u>The sex or physical contact I have before marriage will not affect my marriage relationship.</u>

Sex is a covenant. When the penis penetrates the vagina during virgin sex, the breaking of the hymen and subsequent bloodshed symbolizes the blood Jesus shed on the cross to make a covenant with His church. When two people, Christian or not, engage in intercourse, their spirits are united and bonded. (Have you ever wondered why certain girls remain so attached to guys they slept with, even if the guys are complete losers?) This has a great deal to do with the release of blood which establishes a covenant type of relationship that goes directly to the heart of the woman. A woman's heart and her sexual organs are connected which can cause her emotional trouble even years later. A man's sexual organs are connected to his head leaving his heart free allowing him to completely forget about the encounter.

Research indicates that people who live together prior to getting married are more likely to have marriages that end in divorce. Dr. Phil *The Boston Herald*, Annual Review of Sociology *http://www.drphil.com/articles/article/351*: April 10, 2014

A recent study on cohabitation concluded that after five to seven years, only 21 percent of unmarried couples were still living together. *The downside of living together before you get married, May 28, 2012 by Fr Stephen Wang: http://bridgesandtangents.wordpress.com/2012/0 5/28/the-downside-of-living-together-before-you-get-married/: April 14, 2014*

Now, God can and will cleanse your past sins if you repent and allow Him to clean up your spirit. However, this is a process that often isn't completed without persistent commitment to being changed and healed. All of that is to say that no one should enter in to physical relationships thinking that his or her marriage will not be affected. Everyone who has done such things must aggressively seek the Lord for full restoration.

2. Sex will not be good or satisfying in marriage if both the husband and wife are virgins. The man needs "experience," or we need to "try each other out" first.

Believe it or not, there are many couples who kept themselves for one another and enjoy very fulfilling sex lives. When you begin as virgins together, it really does get better every time. God will not lead you to marry someone and then make you sexually incompatible with that person! That is not to say that some people don't have problems in bed. Dr. Larry Crabb, in his book, *The Marriage Builder*, describes the three types of sexual problems married couples can have.

The first is personal problems, which an individual has emotionally or spiritually, that are usually rooted in past issues. The second is relationship problems, when the husband and wife are having trouble getting along, and this will definitely affect sex. The third is problems with technique, i.e., not "knowing what to do." Dr. Crabb, who has counseled countless couples, states that this last type is by far the easiest to fix.

Sex is not the essence of marriage, just one of its many elements. Its purpose is to first glorify God by uniting husband and wife and producing godly offspring, then to allow the husband and wife to give one another godly, physical pleasure. The pursuit of pleasure for its own sake is always fruitless and causes deeper issues such as guilt and shame and is proven to be far more unsatisfying than a marital relationship.

One of the most comprehensive studies on the subject, which was released in 2010 by the Center for Sexual Health Promotion, confirmed this. At Indiana University, more than 5,800 people took part in the study, which covered the sexual habits of people between ages of 14 and 94.

An average of 61 percent of singles reported that they hadn't had sex within the past year, compared with 18 percent of married people.

They found that 25 percent of married people between 25 and 59 and considered in the prime of life, were still having sex two to three times per week, versus less than five percent of singles in the same age group.

Dr. Larimore, who wrote the book, *His Brain, Her Brain: How Divinely Designed Differences Can Strengthen Your Marriage,* concluded that:

"Sex is better in marriage"

"Sex is better among religious or spiritual couples"

"Sex is not better if you cohabitate"

Remaining a virgin until marriage gives both spouses a wonderful sense of security. Do you really want your spouse to be able to run into someone else that you have slept with? As far as "knowing what to do" on your wedding night, when the time comes, both you and your future spouse can meet (separately of course) with church counselors or your parents to discuss the details, and there are also some books which may be helpful.

3. <u>Sexual sin is defined exclusively by vaginal penetration</u>.

The standard for morality in our generation is so low that we are often seduced into thinking that as long as we don't "go all the way" we're okay in God's eyes. More than a few Christians can give long "biblical" dissertations on how, "The Bible doesn't say you can't kiss, etc." Let's examine this myth for a minute. Kissing, fondling, caressing and all the rest were invented by God to prepare our bodies for sexual intercourse. That is why, during these activities, men get an erection and women become wet in the vaginal area. Why would God want us to engage in activities that prepare our bodies for something He has forbidden?

Obviously, if you aren't dating or spending inappropriate amounts of time with members of the opposite sex, such things will not be an issue. When you do begin courting, a good guideline for physical contact is not to do anything you wouldn't feel comfortable doing in front of your father, or in the church service. Anything you need to do in private should be reserved for the privacy of your marriage bed.

Then there are the people who think that their organs were designed to be stimulated through masturbation and other devices that can bring them to an orgasmic release. The Bible does directly speak against this practice, indicating that this is a type of worship.

The son of Judah, Onan, was expected to marry his brother's widow, and have sex with her to produce children in his deceased brother's place, but when Onan had intercourse with his wife, he spilled the seed on the ground in protest. This angered the Lord and Onan also died. Many have said this has nothing to do with masturbation, but the bottom line is the wasting of the seed and by doing so it had no ability to produce life.

Can life be produced during masturbation? No! Then you tell me what the difference is and if you think God is pleased.

Also the Bible indicates that our bodies are the temples of the Holy Ghost and that our lives are the purchased possession of the Lord Jesus Christ and we don't even belong to ourselves.

How can we engage in this type of activity without the owner's approval? We can't, so you shouldn't!

MYTHS ABOUT THE BIBLE AND MALE-FEMALE RELATIONSHIPS

1. <u>The Bible's teaching on male/female relationships is sexist and out-dated.</u>

As a Christian, you must be confident that the Bible is relevant to every issue you deal with and that God's way is in your best interest. There are many intellectually fashionable criticisms regarding the Bible's view on male/female relationships, and every other topic for that matter. Without taking the time to deal with all of them, we must understand that God's way does not change. Only people's willingness to adhere to God's way changes because of human unwillingness to adhere to His principles.

In fact, as Solomon declared in Ecclesiastes 1:9 "...there is nothing new under the sun." Nothing is new about people challenging God's moral and spiritual requirements for them. They've been doing it for thousands of years, ever since the fall of man. It is only our youthful arrogance that tries to pass off our sinfulness as "enlightened, modern thinking." Whether people have issues with dating, courtship procedure, or gender roles within the home, people have had problems doing right from Sodom and Gomorrah in the Old Testament, to the

Corinthian church in the New Testament, to the present day. While certain philosophical trends vary from age to age, they carry absolutely no power to transform lives for the better, and are often promoted by people whose lives you would not want to emulate.

2. It is too difficult (virtually impossible) to live according to God's standard for my life.

God is the one who is for us and Satan is the one who is against us. Satan wants us to believe we can't do it, so that we will not even try. However, to even subconsciously agree with the devil's lie would be to say that God is not powerful enough to enable us to live the holy and successful life He has called us to! Remember the promise to the Corinthians: "No temptation has overtaken you except such as is common to man; but God is faithful, who will not allow you to be tempted beyond what you are able, but with the temptation will also make the way of escape, that you may be able to bear it." (*1 Corinthians 10:13*)

There are no "super saints," only people who have repented of their sins and given their lives to the Lord. Most people have trouble living for God because they simply don't want to be like Jesus. Every one of us, from Paul the Apostle to the biggest backslider, is given the same opportunity to obey with success. To whom much is given, much is required. If you had a great family background and didn't have to deal with certain sins, great! God expects you to take that blessing and build on it. If you were a product of rape and a victim of abuse, then God has no smaller plans for your life. He'll give you grace to work through the pain, and take you on to heights you can't imagine.

3. If I've already had sex or dated a lot, I am disqualified from conducting myself according to God's standard for my life.

This is the biggest lie of all. None of us are born holy; we can only be made holy by God. To enter the sanctification process does not require that we were raised in a perfect Christian home, or that we have never committed some type of civil crime. It only requires that we repent of our sins and give our lives to Jesus.

If you've had sex or dated around a lot, and you feel "marked," as if you'll never be qualified to become a holy, passionate servant of the Lord, THINK AGAIN. The type of "holiness" that comes from pride in not having "done" anything is called self-righteousness. The type of holiness that comes from repentance and sanctification is called true righteousness. Remember these verses:

"Therefore I say to you, her sins, which are many, are forgiven, for she loved much. But to whom little is forgiven, the same loves little." (*Luke 7:47*)

"Therefore, if anyone is in Christ, he is a new creation. Old things have passed away, behold, all things have become new! (*2 Corinthians 5: 17*)

Live a life in Christ that is free from guilt and shame with the confidence that a loving God has called and empowered you to live successfully. Don't allow the lies that so many unmarried people do to live rent free inside your head to shape your relationships with God and man.

Live a life above reproach!

From Friendship to Courtship

In this chapter, we will outline the basic procedure for the godly transition from being unmarried to marriage. Even if you are not close to the season of your life when you will be married, it is important to know what a biblical courtship looks like. Many ministries have different philosophies about the involvement of spiritual leadership in the courtship process, ranging from a completely hands-off approach, to a legalistic and controlling regimen. Neither extreme is healthy, and should not characterize your church. We are presenting what we believe to be a moderate approach, which will vary somewhat in its application, depending on church leadership style.

As you read through the steps that follow, it is important that you evaluate yourself and be willing to change any and all things which can hinder or have hindered your ability to move from being unmarried to being happily married.

Let's get started!

STEP 1: ATTRACTION

Most relationships that lead to marriage develop initially in the context of normal life. Attraction may be present immediately due to someone's appearance or personality, or it may develop over time, when people discover common interests or outlooks on life. It is important to understand that God has put the tendency to be attracted to members of the opposite sex in us as part of His design. Feeling drawn to someone is not a sin, but neither is it a sure sign that the relationship is to be pursued outside of the context of friendship. During your unmarried life, many potential attractions may come and go, but only one will end in marriage. Handle your emotions wisely; don't let them handle you. If you are prone to jumping into relationships quickly, then it is very important to have a person in your life who can help you walk through the landmine of human attraction. Talk to someone over you who is not one of your peers or someone you are mentoring. Control your thinking process and don't allow yourself to build a fantasy relationship before there is even a hint of compatibility. You will also need an overseer if attractions cause you to run like a cat in a room full of rocking chairs. Attraction can be the first step, but it can also be the step where everything is messed up! Handle this beginning with the care of carrying a box full of china on a slippery floor.

STEP 2: PRAYER

Beginning to actually pray about someone as a potential mate is a very serious step. Any prayer time of this nature that goes beyond just putting a matter of attraction in God's hands should only be entered into if (l) you are confident that it is the right season for you to begin contemplating marriage, and (2) the attraction has lasted for a significant amount of time. (3) You are willing to be told they are not the one. This way you won't become a Christian who wants God to overpower another person's will. If your attraction does not meet these requirements, the best thing you can do is simply put it on the altar before God and go on about your life as normal, largely ignoring it. Praying about someone in the wrong season of your life will only distract you from what God is trying to do with you. Praying extensively about someone whom you've only noticed for a short period of time only prevents the attraction from potentially going away on its own.

When you develop a love for someone whom you believe qualifies for marriage, pray about it in full submission to the will of God. **Don't just talk to God about the person; listen to what He is saying to you.** It is only the grace of God that reveals the contents of our own hearts to us. Ask Him to reveal your inner motivations and to guide you as to whether this is the right person you should be thinking about.

STEP 3: OBTAINING COUNSEL FROM LEADERSHIP

If you have prayed and you believe that God has approved your heart toward this person, seek the counsel of mature Christians who are your elders.

Remember, there already is a person over you who has spoken into this situation before the prayer process started. But now it is time to involve people who can put an immediate stop to the possible relationship. This may be your parents, or those who have been commissioned into leadership in the church. Let me state again: avoid speaking your heart to peers, since this is a serious decision, and you don't want rumors to get around prematurely.

Once you receive godly counsel, it is important for you to follow it. Their perspective will help you move ahead at a safe speed, and is God's way of protecting you from hurting yourself or someone else unnecessarily.

STEP 4: SPEAKING TO YOUR PROSPECTIVE MATE

This step is where procedures change for men and women. Women who sense an attraction, have prayed and sought counsel, must continue to commit the matter to prayer. Where God hasn't told them otherwise, they simply go on about their lives as normal. Men may be counseled to do exactly the same thing, or, if their elders are comfortable with it, they may express their heart to a certain degree to their prospective mate.

Biblically, the man is the proper initiator of the courtship process, because it is a man's job to find a wife, not a woman's job to find a husband (see

Proverbs 18:22). This is seen further in the fact that man and wife are to represent Christ and the Church, and Jesus made it clear that "You did not choose Me, but I chose you..." (*John 15:18; 13:18*)

A man who decides to express his heart to a woman whom he sees as a potential wife must do so with the fear of the Lord. He must carefully weigh the words he uses, taking responsibility before God for the affect they may have on the person to whom they are said. If the feelings are reciprocated, they can then meet with leadership together, and discuss how to proceed. If the woman is uncertain about her feelings, or simply uninterested, they can meet separately with leadership to ensure the preservation of the friendship, and to prevent unnecessary hurt feelings or humiliation.

There are times when a man or woman develop an attraction for his/her wife/husband before the other notices, but there are many more cases when the person has declared that God has given them their mate, and that person has gone on to marry someone else. Did God or the person make a mistake? Neither! This has a great deal to do with a person skipping steps 2 and 3 of the process and thinking that the other person is feeling and thinking the way they are. Fantasy!

STEP 5: OBTAINING THE BLESSING OF THE PARENTS

When the couple is in agreement about working toward the goal of marriage and is ready to make the relationship public, they should obtain the blessing of both sets of parents. The man should speak to the woman's father to ask permission to enter into courtship with his daughter. The woman should meet her potential in-laws and begin to develop a relationship with them. **If any of the parents have an objection, seek the counsel of church leadership.** Generally, it is important to wait until both families are enthusiastic about being joined as a product of the marriage; however, there are exceptions where the parents' will may be over-ridden. Use wisdom.

The point where a formal engagement will occur varies from culture to culture and ministry to ministry. An engagement ring must be purchased in some circles; in others, a family heirloom may be used. Follow the customs of your family and church as much as you can, out of respect.

The older people are when entering a relationship, the more they think that pastoral or parental oversight is unnecessary, yet the Bible doesn't given any age limit for the need of mentoring and counseling. There are many mature Christians in dead-end relationships that, in their rush toward marriage, have broken the biblical principles of morality. Don't allow the pride of age to cloud your understanding of the Word of God and all that is proved for each of us to be successful in everything that we do. This could even mean allowing a parent or parent figure to give their full opinion about the visibly flawed areas. Sometimes this is very difficult for men to do, since they often think it a sign of weakness to confide in others. When you read the bible it is full of men who receive instructions and guidance throughout their lives and were given great responsibility as a result. If you are a man, be one of those men today!

I have told many women not to marry a man who doesn't have another man in his life who tells him, "NO!" This is because men tend not to listen to women the same way they listen to men and believe me; men need regular coaching through life. A wife usually has to move outside of the character of God to get him to listen.

STEP 6: ENTERING INTO PRE-MARITAL COUNSELING

The goal of pre-marital counseling is to ensure a sound biblical foundation for your marriage. It should provide a safe environment for you and your future mate to get to know one another, and to get your individual expectations and apprehensions about marriage out on the table ahead of time. Lack of pre-marital counseling does not mean that a God-ordained marriage is doomed because God, not man, is the author of marriage; however, proper counseling will help ease the transition from singlehood to marriage, and prevent unnecessary struggles, especially in the early years.

Topics that you will discuss during counseling sessions include broad subjects such as your personal spiritual lives, your calling and career goals, and raising children. You will have opportunities to talk about your past, including past relationships you may have had, your relationship with your parents, and their marriages. You will also walk through more practical details involved in beginning life together, such as a budget for your wedding ceremony, a budget and financial goals for your first years together, obtaining housing, and the division of domestic duties. Close to the time of your wedding, you will get counseling regarding your future sexual relationship.

During the counseling session, you may discover that you did not hear God accurately, and that this person is not meant to be your spouse. This is the best time to discover that, if you were unable to hear it in prayer. It is best to speak privately to the person who has been counseling you and then determine how to speak to the other person.

In most cases, the counselor will first attempt to walk you through what may be just nerves and will pray about the situation before revealing it to the other person. Most of the time, this may be overcome and the marriage will take place without any further issues; however, sometimes there are too many differences for a young couple to navigate, and the wedding should be pushed back.

The long-term success of the marriage is the most important issue and not the wedding or getting all dressed up to take pictures that won't mean a thing if the union fails.

CONDUCT DURING COURTSHIP

Courtship should be an exciting and special time, characterized not only by a growing love for one another, but by innocent hearts toward God. Betrothed couples are still only brother and sister, so kissing and other sexual contact is unacceptable. This does not mean there will not be sexual attraction between the two, but it does mean that they must guard their conduct, making sure that temptation cannot get the better of them. One practical way to do this is to agree on a curfew after which they will not be out together, or even talk on the phone during certain hours. There should be accountability for the curfew with parents or counselors. I know, this sounds old fashioned and can even seem to be unrealistic. But the issue is God's standard and not a worldly standard. So much time can be spent together through all of the different mediums available that everyone and everything else suffers.

Make sure that in your newfound love and the business of wedding plans, you do not become isolated from your other friends. Although your spouse becomes your best friend, God has not ordained all our fellowship needs to be met by one person. You need your friends now more than ever, and they will want to share this exciting time with you. Spending time with your future mate and other friends is also a wonderful way to fellowship and avoid temptation at the same time.

During your courtship, become a student of marriage and parenting, in the Word and through books written by men and women of God. Your counselors should give you a reading list that you and your future spouse can enjoy together. Studying the Word and reading books together is a great way to get to know your mate on a spiritual level, and to set healthy patterns to be continued in your marriage.

The Purpose of Your Wedding

The traditional wedding ceremony has lost a lot of its original meaning in our present generation. Couples who have slept together and even lived together have "Christian" ceremonies with a pastor or priest officiating. What was originally intended by God to be a public declaration of a covenant and a visible symbol of His Son's return has been reduced to an excuse to throw an expensive party.

Some couples may feel that they do not need to go through the formality of a ceremony to be married, while others are content to live together without ever having a wedding. Some Christians get into such a deep level of deception that they believe that they don't need a wedding to be married in the eyes of God. While most understand that this is ridiculous, it's important that we understand the purpose of the wedding ceremony itself and why we need it.

A PUBLIC DECLARATION OF A COVENANT

Just like water baptism is a public declaration of an inward commitment to give one's life to Jesus, a wedding is a public declaration of a couple's commitment to give their lives to one another, and become one. The guests are present not just to participate in the festivities, but to witness these vows and be in agreement with them.

The Apostles preached that we are to repent and be baptized (*Acts 2:38*) in order to enter into a relationship with God. In the same way, our commitment to our spouse means nothing if we are not willing to make it public and legally binding.

A VISIBLE SYMBOL OF JESUS' RETURN FOR THE CHURCH

Marriage itself is meant to visibly represent in the earth the relationship that Jesus has with His Church (*Ephesians 5:25-29*). In the same way, the marriage of believers symbolizes the Marriage Supper of the Lamb, which will occur when Jesus returns to the earth for His Church. God instituted marriage and the wedding procedure in the Hebrew culture in a way that would speak to the culmination of history. Here is an overview of a traditional Jewish wedding and the corresponding Scripture passages describing Jesus' relationship to the Church.

The Betrothal Process

The man is responsible to God to find you; it shouldn't be the other way around. It is ok to pray for God to lead the man to the place that he can find you, and since you can fully trust the Lord, you can destroy your checklist.

If anyone should have the checklist, it is the one searching for the treasure, not the treasure!

Ye have not chosen me, but I have chosen you, and ordained you, that ye should go and bring forth fruit, and that your fruit should remain: that whatsoever ye shall ask of the Father in my name, he may give it you. John 15:16

The Arrangement

The father of the bride is very important to the process of keeping the proper value on the woman. If a natural father is not in the picture, a spiritual father or father figure must take his place. One of the major problems with fathers being removed out of society is that it devalues their daughters in the eyes of their pursuers.

The process isn't a dating process but a courtship process, and for it to be done in a proper fashion, a father is needed to speak with the man like a man. Everything that takes place in this process is under the supervision of the father. The daughter at this point has the name of her father and must protect his name at all costs.

Once the bride is chosen, then the two men agree on the price required for the potential bridegroom to have the daughter's hand in marriage.

Notice that she isn't paying the price, the man is! If he is broke, then there is no marriage. They can tell the father all about how much they are in love, but the father must keep the value of his daughter before the eyes of the man. The father knows that what a man has to commit to and purchase carries a greater value in his heart. This is one of the reasons that once the man has pre-marital sex with a woman, he has no other need for her, since what he valued was sex and that is now off of his list. The price agreement secures the fact that this woman isn't going to be touched until she is fully valued.

For you were bought at a price; therefore glorify God in your body and in your spirit, which are God's. 1 Corinthians 6:20

...knowing that you were not redeemed with corruptible things, like silver or gold, from your aimless conduct received by tradition from your fathers, but with the precious blood of Christ, as of a lamb without blemish and without spot. 1 Peter 1:18-19

The Marriage Contract

Next, there is a covenant agreement between the father, the potential bridegroom, and the bride. The covenant or contract details the husband's obligations to his wife, both in the natural and spiritually. Notice again where the responsibility lies; it is with the husband and not with the wife. When Mrs. Adam was presented to Adam, she had absolutely no needs.

For this is my blood of the new covenant, which is shed for many for the remission of sins. Matthew 26:28

For finding fault with them, he saith, Behold, the days come, saith the Lord, when I will make a new covenant with the house of Israel and with the house of Judah: Hebrews 8:8

Not according to the covenant that I made with their fathers in the day when I took them by the hand to lead them out of the land of Egypt; because they continued not in my covenant, and I regarded them not, saith the Lord. Hebrews 8:9

For this is the covenant that I will make with the house of Israel after those days, saith the Lord; I will put my laws into their mind, and write them in their hearts: and I will be to them a God, and they shall be to me a people: Hebrews 8:10

And they shall not teach every man his neighbour, and every man his brother, saying, Know the Lord: for all shall know me, from the least to the greatest. Hebrews 8:11

For I will be merciful to their unrighteousness, and their sins and their iniquities will I remember no more. Hebrews 8:12

In that he saith, A new covenant, he hath made the first old. Now that which decayeth and waxeth old is ready to vanish away. Hebrews 8:13

<u>The Bride's Consent</u>

With all of this done between the potential husband and the father, the woman must still give her consent. She holds all of the power in that if she doesn't want it, then she is covered by her father and the man has no rights to her. Her father can attempt to persuade her but she has the right of refusal. Therefore, no one can force you to give your life to anyone. It is your choice, and you should only do so when you are properly valued and honored the way you want to be.

...if you confess with your mouth the Lord Jesus and believe in your heart that God has raised Him from the dead, you will be saved. Romans 10:9

Drinking From the Cup (sealing the engagement)

This portion of the marriage tradition is very important and should be observed on a regular basis. Most only participate in the sealing of the engagement during the communion service at church, but Jesus told the disciples that they should do this often. It keeps the church aware of the fact that they are already purchased and married.

Likewise he also took the cup after supper, saying, "This cup is the new covenant in my blood, which is shed for you. Luke 22:20

After the same manner also he took the cup, when he had supped, saying, This cup is the new testament in my blood: this do ye, as oft as ye drink it, in remembrance of me. 1Corinthians 11:25

Bride Receives Gift from the Bridegroom

The main gift the man provides for the woman is the ring. Have you thought about the fact that the only one with a gift before the ceremony is the woman? Valued!

The bride doesn't have to wait for gifts at the marriage celebration because the bridegroom honors her by bringing gifts with him before the ceremony.

This is another example of the value placed on the woman that she should be lavished with gifts.

In whim you also trusted, after you heard the word of truth, the gospel of your salvation; in whom also, having believed, you were sealed with the Holy Spirit of promise, who is the guarantee of our inheritance until the redemption of the purchased possession, to the praise of His glory. Ephesians 1:13-14

But the manifestation of the Spirit is given to each one for the profit of all: for to one is given the word of wisdom through the Spirit, to another the word of knowledge through the same Spirit, to another faith by the same Spirit, to another gifts of healings by the same Spirit, to another the working of miracles, to another prophecy, to another discerning of spirits, to another different kinds of tongues, to another the interpretation of tongues. 1 Corinthians 12:7-10

The Washing of the Bride (Sanctification)

This is a very important process that involves the woman only and doesn't require any other person's help. Completely nude, she is to enter a water source that is running or moving. She must submerge her entire body under the water several times and repeat the blessing for immersion.

When the believer repents of their sins (Washing of Water) and is found in Christ (Immersion), then that person has now joined the Christ as His bride.

Then Peter said to them, "Repent, and let every one of you be baptized in the name of Jesus Christ for the remission of sins; and you shall receive the gift of the Holy Spirit. Acts 2:38

Husbands, love your wives, just as Christ also loved the church and gave Himself for her, that He might sanctify and cleanse her with the washing of water by the word, that He might present her to Himself a glorious church, not having spot or wrinkle or any such thing, but that she should be holy and without blemish. Ephesians 5:25-27

Bridegroom Prepares a Place

In my Father's house are many mansions; if it were not so, I would have told you. I go to prepare a place for you. And if I go and prepare a place for you, I will come again and receive you to myself; that where I am, there you may be also. John 14:2-3

Many people have wondered why Jesus couldn't stay after the resurrection and set up His kingdom at that time. It would have solved a great deal of problems, since the enemy was defeated, death *and the grave was defeated, and mankind could reclaim its rightful place.*

Jesus had to leave so the marriage would be completed and to add value to the church (bride) He would marry. It is the husband who goes away to provide for the wife so that she can simply enter into her possession. As I mentioned earlier, the weight of the entire process is on the husband's shoulders because it is his wedding and she is the very valuable crown that he found.

Consecration of the Bride

The bride is set apart for her husband and no one else can lay claim to her. She wears a veil to indicate that she is espoused to another and will soon be joined with Him where He is. The church is set apart and is veiled from the world and all of its advancements that entice it to be entangled in worldly affairs.

Therefore, brethren, having boldness to enter the Holiest by the blood of Jesus, by a new and living way which he consecrated for us, through the veil, that is, His flesh, and having a High Priest over the house of God, let us draw near with a true heart in full assurance of faith, having our hearts sprinkled from an evil conscience and our bodies washed with pure water. Let us hold fast the confession of our hope without wavering, for he who promised is faithful. And let us consider one another in order to stir up love and good works, not forsaking the assembling of ourselves together, as is the manner of some, but exhorting one another, and so much the more as you see the day approaching. Hebrews 10:19-25

<u>The Return of the Bridegroom</u>

The Bible teaches that Christ will return for His bride the church at the appointed time of the Father. It is the father's responsibility to instruct the bridegroom in the preparation. Once the home meets the standard of the father, the bridegroom can then go to receive his bride into her new home.

And he said unto them, It is not for you to know the times or the seasons, which the Father hath put in his own power. Acts 1:7

Let not your heart be troubled: ye believe in God, believe also in me. In my Father's house are many mansions: if it were not so, I would have told you. I go to prepare a place for you. And if I go and prepare a place for you, I will come again, and receive you unto myself; that where I am, there ye may be also. And whither I go ye know, and the way ye know. John 14:1-4

Therefore, brethren, having boldness to enter the Holiest by the blood of Jesus, by a new and living way which He consecrated for us, through the veil, that is, His flesh, and having a High Priest over the house of God, let us draw near with a true heart in full assurance of faith, having our hearts sprinkled from an evil conscience and our bodies washed with pure water. Let us hold fast the confession of our hope without wavering, for He who promised is faithful. And let us consider one another in order to stir up love and good works, not forsaking the assembling of ourselves together, as is the manner of some, but exhorting one another, and so much the more as you see the Day approaching. Hebrews 10:19-25

In the same way, the church is waiting for the return of Christ and He must wait for the Father to release Him to return. There is some debate on how and when this will happen, but the entire church is sure He is coming for His bride and the wedding ceremony confirms that fact.

<u>The Procession Back to the Father's House</u>

The bridegroom doesn't re-enter the father's house, but stands outside and calls for the bride. She is waiting for his return and is keeping a lamp burning in the window to indicate that. Her bridesmaids help her to get ready and she leaves her father's house and is joined to her husband with torches and oil lambs burning. The bride is placed on a blanket, lifted from the ground, carried, and celebrated by all who witness the parade.

But I would not have you to be ignorant, brethren, concerning them which are asleep, that ye sorrow not, even as others which have no hope. For if we believe that Jesus died and rose again, even so them also which sleep in Jesus will God bring with him. For this we say unto you by the word of the Lord, that we which are alive and remain unto the coming of the Lord shall not prevent them which are asleep. For the Lord himself shall descend from heaven with a shout, with the voice of the archangel, and with the trump of God: and the dead in Christ shall rise first: Then we which are alive and remain shall be caught up together with them in the clouds, to meet the Lord in the air: and so shall we ever be with the Lord. Wherefore comfort one another with these words.
1Thessalonians 4:13-18

These are scriptures that are used mostly at funerals but they are really another part of the wedding ceremony. Once a person is a part of the church, then it doesn't matter if they are dead or alive; they will make the procession from this world to the Father.

"And at midnight a cry was heard: 'Behold, the bridegroom is coming; go out to meet him!' Then all those virgins arose and trimmed their lamps.

And the foolish said to the wise, 'Give us some of your oil, for our lamps are going out.' But the wise answered, saying, 'No, lest there should not be enough for us and you; but go rather to those who sell, and buy for yourselves.' And while they went to buy, the bridegroom came, and those who were ready went in with him to the wedding; and the door was shut. Matthew 25:6-10

If the bride isn't ready and her lamp isn't burning in her window, then she could be left behind!

<u>The Consummation</u>

All of the ceremonial things are exciting and rewarding, but the actual marriage isn't sealed until the two people come together in intercourse. Remember, the woman is holding the blood seal to the marriage.

This is very important to her father because this will also indicate her faithfulness to him and to his name. Usually, the virgin will have her hymen broken and blood will be released, sealing the marriage covenant, but also indicating that she is a virgin. If there is no blood, then the marriage is over and the dowry given to the father must be returned. She must be spotless and pure for the marriage to be complete. This is a seven day process where the couple is separated from the guests. Upon their return, the blood stained sheet is presented to the father of the bride to indicate her faithfulness to him.

Husbands, love your wives, even as Christ also loved the church, and gave himself for it; That he might sanctify and cleanse it with the washing of water by the word, That he might present it to himself a glorious church, not having spot, or wrinkle, or any such thing; but that it should be holy and without blemish. Ephesians 5:25-27

Once the believer has come to know Christ, they must do everything in their power under the direction of the Holy Spirit to remain clean for the bridegroom.

<u>*The Marriage Supper*</u>

When the couple returns to the guests, they will share another cup of wine.

Let us be glad and rejoice and give Him glory, for the marriage of the Lamb has come, and His wife has made herself ready." Revelation 19:7

But I say to you, I will not drink of this fruit of the vine from now on until that day when I drink it new with you in My Father's kingdom." Matthew 26:29

There are many who have indicated that it is okay to drink a little wine even once you have become a

Christian, and many do. I have always held the position that if Jesus isn't going to drink again until I am one with Him, then I will not allow any wine or strong drink to enter my mouth either.

I want the wedding ceremony to be completed in the way He has designed it to be.

Do You Really Want to Get Married?

Marriage has a cost associated with it, just like salvation, and like salvation, we must count that cost before entering into it. A commitment is not a commitment unless you understand and have weighed what it will require of you. Anything less is an impulsive, empty promise, often leading to feelings of resentment and bitterness. Of course, we can never know the full implications of this life-changing decision ahead of time even with all of the preparation that should take place before the marriage. Jesus is simple; He asks for everything. Marriage will require no less. Here are some thoughts to consider:

Have I done everything I want to do while I'm unmarried? Am I willing to give up whatever I haven't done?

Am I ready to give up the freedom and flexibility associated with my being unmarried?

Have I made the most of my being unmarried? Has God been pleased with my conduct and accomplishments?

Am I ready to prefer another's needs over my own as a constant way of life?

Do I live a financially responsible life now? Do I have a track record of making sound financial decisions?

Have I gotten to know God well enough in my own spiritual life, so that even if God took my spouse from me, I would continue to serve Him?

Do I consistently cultivate the presence of God to a degree that I could carry not only myself, but a household?

Am I a good friend to the friends I have now?

Am I characterized by quickly resolving conflicts with people, particularly family members? Do I consistently pursue the Lord to work through personal issues?

Would I describe myself as a whole and complete, mature man or woman of God?

Do I have a strong witness in my heart from the Lord that this is the season of my life when I should be contemplating marriage?

MYTHS ABOUT MARRIAGE

Christians have unfortunately embraced a lot of the world's standards when it comes to marriage as an institution. Here are few lies of the enemy that we must be delivered from to live successfully as an unmarried Christian, and later in marriage:

1. (For Women) <u>There aren't enough good men out there, so I have to lower my standard.</u>

The problem of lowering the standard appears to be more of an issue with women, but the same principles apply to men who want a godly wife. Ideally, your father should have been a sufficient model of Christian manhood that you would have no desire to lower your standard. Unfortunately, such fathers are not always to be found, and thus many men don't know how to be men of God and many women don't know how to distinguish what a man of God looks like. As God reveals His standard to you as an unmarried woman, it has direct implications for the man you will marry.

Most Christian women would never come right out and say that they don't believe God is capable of providing a godly husband for them. However, that is exactly what we are saying when we lower our standard and are willing to accept an offer from someone on whom God is not smiling. If you marry someone with the internal conviction that you are "settling for the best you can get," you are giving your marriage a lot of unnecessary and unnatural problems right from the start. Women owe it to their husbands to respect them and look up to them spiritually, so don't marry someone you don't feel that way about.

2. <u>I can't wait around anymore; I need to go find someone for myself</u>.

You cannot predict when you will get married. Some marry at twenty-two, others at forty-two. The season of your life for marriage is determined sovereignly by God. You cannot rush it or delay it and stay in His will. Many times it is out of His mercy that He doesn't answer prayers to alter His perfect timing, which is set in His infinite wisdom.

It can be very challenging, given some of the cultural pressure to get married, especially for certain women who remain unmarried as they get a little older. However, you will never get anything good by stepping out of God's way of doing things. There are tremendous rewards for those who will wait on the Lord, even in the face of outside pressure, for His perfect will.

3. <u>I can compromise as an unmarried man or woman and expect my children to have a higher standard</u>.

The ultimate form of this myth is found in the father who had sex with his girlfriend before they were married and yet expects no one to touch his daughter. Still, many women who violated their consciences as teens in anything from outright fornication, to just sneaking out of their houses, now find themselves yelling at their daughters to stop doing the very same things! It is your spirit, not just your words, that is reproduced in your disciples, and your number one disciples will be your children.

Of course, if we repent of sin and allow God to clean up our spirits, we can pass along a much better inheritance to our precious children. However, whenever we do anything against God while knowing better, we automatically open doors of evil that will affect our children. Whenever you are challenged to hold up God's standard for yourself, think of your future daughter, and how you would want her to behave. Women, would you want her out late at night with a man? Would you want her revealing intimate emotions to a man? Would you want her wearing what you wear? Men, would you want a man to treat your daughter the way you treat women? Would you entrust your daughter to someone like yourself? Think about this, and carry yourself in a way that you can be proud to display to your heavenly Father.

4. Marriage equals emotional and financial security.

Children do not get married, adults do. Children, by definition, need parents to take care of them. Adults, by definition, are able to take care of themselves. While the husband must be able to spiritually, emotionally, and financially support his family, the wife is not another child he needs to take care of. While wives are meant to capably help their husbands, husbands are not supposed to be helpless invalids who can't cook and clean for themselves.

If you are still lonely and unfulfilled in God alone, marriage will not solve your problems. If you are financially irresponsible and inconsistent in managing your own money, marriage will frequently makes it worse. In fact, getting married in such a state can put so many unrealistic expectations on the relationship, that it will be quite a while before you actually experience security. Stability and security come from one's relationship with God, family, and church family, and are prerequisites for marriage. Your stability in God should couple with your future husband's to produce a wonderfully secure environment for your children.

5. I can have a successful marriage without deliberately working toward that goal, by just going with the flow of society.

If you want to be financially successful, you may have to change your spending habits. If you want to be academically successful, you may have to change your study habits. If you want a successful marriage, you may have to change your social habits. It's just that simple.

Most people marry today expecting marital bliss to shower down on them automatically. However, the reality is that half of the marriages in America break up, and the statistics are the same for Christians and non-Christians. Of those who stay together, even more are not successfully glorifying God by demonstrating Jesus' relationship with the church in their marriage. So if the vast majority of our society, Christian and non-Christian, is not successfully glorifying God in their marriages, then we must be willing to go against the flow of mainstream society, and mainstream Christian society, for the sake of a successful marriage and family.

This call to go against the flow applies to your conduct in your unmarried life as we have discussed, but also to your conduct in your future marriage. Although there are some sensible books that may help you in the future, your best bet is to learn about this by spending time with successfully married, Christian couples, not by attending hundreds of marriage seminars! Their examples and insight will be far more valuable than all the "marriage experts" put together.

A Godly Vision for Marriage

Gender roles within the family vary greatly from one society to another, and have changed in the United States tremendously in the last fifty years. As Christians, it is essential that we seek to understand God's vision for the family as He intended it to be from the beginning. God's Word is not silent on the issue of family structure, and His instructions are not optional. It is impossible to understand what God truly intends for husbands and wives to be if we succumb even a little to the relativistic ethics of our generation. The obliteration of specific roles within the home is the foundational philosophy for feminism, homosexuality, and the ultimate destruction of the family itself.

When we step outside of God's original intent for the family through our decisions, we step away from His blessings and are forced to try to make things work in our own strength. When we embrace our God-given role within the family He gives us, we will be overwhelmed by His blessings. The choice is ours.

WHAT IS A HUSBAND?

God has set up husbands as the leader in the family unit. Just as a country only has one president and a state only has one governor, the family only has one head. As the one God placed in charge, *the husband is responsible for the spiritual, emotional, and financial health of his family.* Even if he has delegated the responsibility to keep the checkbook to his wife, God holds him responsible for the family's financial state. Although the wife may be the one at home with the children during the day, he is responsible to train them, and to provide direction and support for his wife. This becomes even more important when both husband and wife have full-time jobs and the children spend their day in daycare or after-school programs.

All biblical requirements of leadership apply to husbands, including the charge in John 13 and Matthew 23:11 to be the greatest servant. Servanthood should characterize all godly husbands.

Listed below are some of the major responsibilities of husbands, for which God will hold them accountable. All men who are married or believe they are entering the season of life to be married must embrace these responsibilities. If they do, they will find that

God empowers them to successfully lead their home and bring Him glory in the earth. To despise or neglect these responsibilities is to violate God's will, and misrepresent Him to his family and the world.

The priest and spiritual leader of the home

God has ordained for husbands to be the head of the household, leading by character and example, as well as by giving verbal guidance (see Ephesians 5:23). Too many families survive on the wife's prayer life alone. A husband's leadership is demonstrated not only in prayer and his understanding of the Word of God, but by the fact that he is emotionally mature and stable. He should not be characterized by responding to challenges with his wife or children out of his emotions, but out of an understanding of God's heart.

He takes responsibility before God for his family's spiritual condition and direction. He sees them as his most important disciples, and gives them first place in his life. He loves to be around them, and is always happy to come home. He initiates corporate prayer and devotions with his wife and children on a regular basis (daily, or several times a week). No matter how demanding his job is, he will make time to get alone with God, and to make time for his family.

The provider and protector of the home

Just as Jesus provides for all the needs of the church, God has chosen husbands to meet the physical needs of their wives and children, and protect them from any physical or spiritual danger. A husband does not have to bring home a lot of money to be a good provider; he just needs to be responsible with what he does bring home. Most couples who get into debt make sufficient money, but overspend. A godly husband has enough self-restraint to wait to purchase things that he might want, because he is more concerned about his family having what they need.

A husband cares for and protects his wife and children as his own body (Ephesians 5:27, 28). He is their spiritual covering and first level of accountability. He not only listens to his wife, but is alert to her spiritual, emotional, and physical condition. Because he knows her strengths and weaknesses, he watches out for ways the enemy may be attacking her through discouragement, fatigue, or outside influences. When he feels she needs something, such as prayer time with him, time away to pray on her own, or a nice dinner or a new blouse, he makes sure she can get it. He will not passively watch his children grow up, but will actively shape their character by instruction, correction, and rebuke. He will monitor their progress in every area of their lives, knowing their likes, dislikes, talents, and weaknesses.

The captain of the family team

As the head of the house, the husband is receiving vision not just for his own life, but for his team, which is his family. Our society has become so individualistic that family members live more like strangers under the same roof instead of embracing the corporate purpose God has for them as a team. The husband's ability to hear God for that corporate purpose and to articulate it effectively and consistently to his wife and children is crucial to the success of the family unit. A wife should never have to ask, "What is the Lord showing you?" or "Where are we heading as a family?" because he should be talking with her and getting her input at all times. When children come, they are not made to feel as burdensome hotel guests, but like welcome, needed members of the team.

A submitted man of God

The worst thing for anyone is to be submitted to someone who is not submitted himself. Jesus, the model for all husbands, was submitted to the Father. God does not only require that a wife submit to her husband, but that the husband is submitted to God, spiritual leadership, and walks in mutual submission with his wife. (Ephesians 5:2 1) His heart models submission for children to imitate, and keeps the home in order.

Questions to consider about a potential husband:

1. Am I willing to leave everything to follow this man the way I left everything to follow Jesus?

2. Do I look up to and respect this man's relationship with God and trust his submission to his leaders?

3. Do I understand and believe in this man's vision enough to devote my time, energy, and talents to help him bring it to pass?

4. Do I believe this man will be a godly and loving father who will nurture and train our children faithfully?

5. Do I love this man unconditionally?

WHAT IS A WIFE?

To many people today, the term "wife" means little more than being a man's roommate. Most young people today seem to think that good women are a dime a dozen, but that a good man is really hard to find. This tends to give men a false sense of confidence, thinking they have plenty to choose from, and frequently makes women feel that they need to lower their standards. The Bible does not agree. God tells us, "Who can find a virtuous wife? Her worth is far above rubies." (*Proverbs 31*) This describes something that is not only incredibly valuable, but also rare.

A godly wife will not look or act like the average Christian woman-- her standards are much higher. She didn't settle for the same empty lifestyle her hallmates had in college. She doesn't accept society's invitation to let her husband fend for himself and to dump her children on someone else to rear while she pursues her own dreams. She doesn't waste time and brain space with the popular television shows and gossip. She is devoted, hard-working, humble and dependable. The fact that she is so attractive to her husband is not only a result of her physical appearance, but her inward devotion to God, and her willingness to stand by him in anything. Her patience, kindness, and love fill the house with warmth, and her hard work and wisdom keep it in order. All this makes her husband want to rush to get home every day.

To the godly wife, "having it all" does not equate to the world's empty promises of fame, fortune, and fulfillment. It is shocking that most young (and middle-aged) women today believe that careers are fulfilling, but wifehood and motherhood are stressful and difficult. Add to that the financial pressure from employers who do not feel obliged to pay a husband a living wage, and the church's refusal to see unmarried moms as group who needs help and much support as well as the focus that should be on widows the way the Bible charges it to be (1 Timothy 5), and we are close to losing an entire generation of children, Christian and non-Christian, to the world. Does a wife or mom really have to pray to see if it's God's will for her to be at home? Proverbs 31 gives a beautiful portrait of the virtuous wife, declaring her incredible worth. Here are some of her responsibilities:

The capable helper to the husband

A wife's first calling, after being called unto God Himself, is to join her husband in divine worship of God Almighty. Then they are to accomplish the vision for the family that God has given them (Genesis 2:18). As she does this, God's vision for her as an individual will be fulfilled. Women have been deceived into thinking that husbands and children get in the way of their calling. The virtuous wife realizes that her ministry to her husband and children is the God-ordained path to the fullness of

God's will for her, that it builds the character of Christ in her and trains her for leadership in the generation.

A true helper does what she is asked to do, not what she necessarily wants to do all the time. Although the husband is the spiritual leader of the home, God has given her the ability to be the perfect complement to him, so they may be equally yoked in every way. She is devoted to helping her husband accomplish what God has laid on their hearts, not to manipulating him into doing what she sees, but what God has perhaps not yet revealed to him.

The provider for the family from within

Though God has not ordained women to be the breadwinners of the family, they certainly are to augment the family's income in many ways. The wife in Proverbs 31 invested money, and sold garments she created. In addition, she cooked and sewed for her household, stretching the dollars her husband brought home. It is very clear that the Proverbs 31 woman is wealthy, but hasn't diminished her husband's role in the family. It is important that the understanding of oneness in the marriage is maintained, which means it doesn't matter who brings home the most money; it is still "them" doing it!

As a national speaker, God has blessed me to earn a good living, but every time I go away my wife goes with me even when she stays home, since we are one. Therefore, all of the earnings belong to her as much as they belong to me. My wife owns her own business selling jewelry and woman's apparel of which I know very little about, but the earnings are as much mine as they are hers.

The manager of the family team

The husband is the head of the home, but the wife is the first one to implement his guidance within it. The wife "watches over the ways of her household and does not eat the bread of idleness." If the wife is at home with the children all day, she must not only train them, but keep her husband informed of their progress. Her prayer and worship life fills the home with the atmosphere of the presence of God, making it a sanctuary to her family and a ministry center to the community. "She extends her hand to the poor, yes, she reaches out her hands to the needy."

Some women I've met have asked me to show them these women who have all of this time in their day. You will be surprised at what happens when you ask God to help you do what He has told you! Time seems to expand, money goes further and life just works better than ever. Father will increase our lives in the simple areas simply because we asked Him. New and exciting doors can and will be open to you from places that no one could have predicted. The other thing you must do is to have a schedule and keep it; your life will thrive and the responsibilities of marriage and family will become much easier.

A submitted woman of God

Submitting to one's husband is a joy to the woman who is secure and knows God for herself. One reason women resist having a submitted heart toward their husbands is that they have been taught that value comes from authority or position, rather than from identity in God. True submission is tested when there is a difference of opinion over a matter. When the marriage relationship is flourishing, submission is rarely arduous, even when there is a small challenge.

Questions to consider about a potential wife:

1. Am I willing to sacrifice everything for this woman the way Jesus sacrificed everything for me?

2. Do I respect and care for this woman enough to give her access to my entire life?

3. Do I believe this woman is capable of helping me to bring my God-given vision to pass?

4. Do I believe this woman will be a capable and loving mother who will nurture and train our children faithfully?

5. Do I love this woman unconditionally?

Summary

Your First Love

When you ask a person about their first love, another *person* will usually come to mind, but for a Christian it should be Father God who comes to mind. The Bible says, "We love him, because he first loved us." (*1 John 4:19*)

This mean that even before our parents were in our lives God loved us, not just through His word, but through His actions.

"For God so loved the world that he gave his only begotten Son, that whosoever believeth in him should not perish, but have everlasting life." (*John 3:16*)

This proves God's love for mankind, that while we were in sin, He sent His Son Jesus to die for our transgressions. Therefore, everything that we do in this life should be in response to that amazing love demonstrated on the cross.

The Bible refers to this as our First Love in the book of Revelation, where God deals with the church at Ephesus.

"Nevertheless I have somewhat against thee, because thou hast left thy first love." (*Revelation 2:4*)

The nursery rhyme from which the title of this book is taken declares that *first comes love*; without a doubt speaking of human love, and it is correct from a natural or a spiritual sense. The rhyme continues with *then comes marriage*, and again this is correct since God's love comes first, then He establishes a marriage covenant between the ones He redeemed through love.

This is why I have used the descriptor *unmarried* instead of *single* throughout this book; a Christian may be alone in the earth, but as do all married Christians, they have a mate in the heavens, too.

It is the responsibility of all believers to cultivate and increase this marital relationship whether married or unmarried in the earth.

All disciplines such as prayer, fasting, study of the word of God, and fellowship among other believers require us to have a relationship with the Lord. The unmarried person must keep all of these disciplines fully functional before God sends the one person into their life who they can join in oneness.

Making the Most of Your Unmarried Life

I encourage unmarried Christians to enjoy their lives and to be intense about their relationship with God. This is a time to enjoy all night prayer, fasting, planned times to get away and many other things.

One problem I find with unmarried Christians is the fact that they are so busy with life that they can't enjoy it. When there is a child involved, the busyness of the unmarried Christian increases exponentially, due to school obligations and child's social development.

Finding someone who can help with the child while you take time to get away or to attend a conference is very important and this is something you should do regularly. Schedule your life and stop allowing life to dictate how you will live and enjoy life. In the Appendix for the *First Comes Love* Workbook, you will find all of the necessary forms you need to start scheduling your life.

It is time for those who are still unmarried to make the most of their time without an earthly mate; this can't happen if all of the attention is placed on getting married because the person feels lonely and unfulfilled.

One of the greatest traps of the enemy is to make a person feel that they need another person in their lives to meet their needs. Paul the Apostle helps us understand exactly who should be meeting every need:

"But my God shall supply all your need according to his riches in glory by Christ Jesus."(*Philippians 4:19*)

Live like God is supplying your needs and enjoy every moment of your life!

Have you discovered your God-given purpose? Your purpose must the driving force of your life, and it is the thing that will help you get up early in the morning and stay up late at night.

All of your family and friends will realize that you have purpose because it will dominate your conversations and attention when you spend time with them. When your purpose is front and center in your heart and mind, sometimes it is difficult to see the need for or to even allow a potential mate into your life.

Always remember both Ruth and Isaac had purpose and each was working as unto the Lord when their mates came into their lives. Purposeful work can be the very thing that causes the mate you have been waiting for to appear.

The unmarried must live their purpose and keep their eyes open for the right person!

Your Growing Relationship with Your Parents

Some of the most important people to help with your purpose and help you determine if this is the right life mate for you are natural and/or spiritual parents. Too many unmarried people miss the value of parents, especially when they are older.

Knowing more than your parents isn't the issue, it is what Father God has placed inside of the parent's heart that the child can't feel. If you have children, then you know how this feeling works in relation to them, but you might forget that it works the same with your parents.

Strained relationships with natural parents mean that spiritual parents are needed so that the parenting process can be intact and functional. There are unmarried women and men my age and younger who look to me as a spiritual parent to help guide them through relationship waters.

Always remember that the first law with promise commands us to obey our parents, whether they are Christians or not. Use the wisdom given to parents in every part of your life, but especially when it concerns your purpose and a potential marital relationship.

As a pastor, there are many times I have counseled a couple having marital problems where one or both set of parents didn't think it was a good idea for the marriage to take place, but when emotions get involved it is very difficult for grown people to hear that kind of old fashioned wisdom.

Hindsight is always twenty-twenty, but it is important to remember that many times parents can see through foresight what children see by hindsight. Learn to respect and trust your parents' wisdom.

Covenant Friendships

Isn't it wonderful how the Bible speaks into areas of life? This fact is true for developing long lasting friendships as well.

"A man that hath friends must shew himself friendly: and there is a friend that sticketh closer than a brother." (*Proverbs 18:24*)

In my time as a pastor, I have discussed with many people the fact that they don't have many friends. Sometimes they even say that being alone is the way they prefer to live.

When an unmarried person makes these statements, I know that this could become a problem if they would like to be married. If we can't make common friends, how can we make lasting romantic friends?

 A husband or wife must be your friend as well as your mate. It is not enough to love the other person, you must also like them.

We grow up developing friends before attaching any romantic overtones to them, so that friendship becomes the foundation of life. During this time, usually girls don't like boys and boys don't like girls.

Both respond the same way to anything other than friendship with each other: "Yuck!"

They are developing friendships among their family and peers, though. God established this so that we will always have someone on whom we can depend and with whom we can share our hearts. Think for a moment, how many people are still your friends from your neighborhood, high school, college or your former city? How many people can you call friend right now in your life, other than family members?

Once a romantic interest develops, if there are no friends then sometimes there is no balance. All of your attention and time is spent focusing on that person and it can be a problem if the other person has a healthy circle of friends with whom they are accustomed to spend time and you want them to spend the majority of their time with you.

If both people have friends, then they can balance their lives between being together and spending time with the people who have been there for them before the romantic relationship began. During the espousal period, I counsel couples to schedule time with family and friends so they don't start to feel left out.

Allow family and friends to enjoy the love developing among them, so that they can celebrate the gift of love with you. Friends are very important and it is the responsibility of the one desiring friendship to be a good friend.

Living Above Reproach

One of the most important things that any Christian can do is to live above reproach and there aren't a lot of places where this message is taught. Christians now think they can go anywhere, do anything, wear whatever they want, and cross most lines and not be judged.

"Let not then your good be evil spoken of." (*Romans 14:16*)

People outside of the church world are always watching Christians to judge their behavior, and it is important to live in the manner the Bible instructs. Isn't interesting that those people who never read the Bible know what Christians should do and how they should behave?

This is one of the reasons they will not be able to say to God that they didn't know what was required because He has placed this understanding in their conscience and will judge them based on it.

"For when the Gentiles, which have not the law, do by nature the things contained in the law, these, having not the law, are a law unto themselves:" (*Romans 2:14*)

All of the different styles, attitudes and things that are popular must be judged in the light of Kingdom reality before we embrace them. This is very important once a potential mate comes into your life; the standard of God must be the first thing they experience from you.

What time may the person come to your home? What time do they have to leave? How close can they sit next to you while visiting? Who knows where you are when you are out alone with this person?

We can ask more questions, but I think you get the picture. Women must hold standards so that the man doesn't start thinking about dirt issues, because it is very easy for men to flip the switch from friend to sex partner without commitment. Don't allow this to take place; make him respect you, and he will desire you even more!

Live your life above reproach and the whole world will acknowledge the Lord in you!

From Friendship to Courtship

A very delicate situation occurs when a friendship transitions from friendship to courtship; if not handled properly, both the potential marital relationship and the friendship may be destroyed.

It is necessary to share your feelings with someone who can help keep everything balanced as soon as

141

possible, but never with the friend or the friend of your friend. Moving forward can be exciting when the other person's heart is really for the relationship to move forward in the same direction.

Remember, standards must immediately be put in place that weren't necessary when this was only a friendship. Certain standards should have been in place even with the friendship relationship but not the courtship standards we discussed before.

Your family and friends are most likely familiar with your friendship, so once the courtship is established and given guidance by a mentoring spiritual leader and one or both of your parents, it is time to share the news with everyone else.

Don't change too much too fast and watch how God can change what was a great friendship into a great marriage.

The Purpose of Your Wedding

So many people have attended a wedding ceremony with absolutely no idea what they are watching.

The ceremony is designed for everyone to understand whose wedding it is and just how valuable the bride is to the husband. Not only are they expressing their love for each other, they are also announcing a new authority in the earth.

The father of the bride gives her away and at the same time releases her from his name and authority. The husband-to-be takes her while she is still under the authority of her father's name, and makes vows to her that please her and her father. The wife-to-be says her vows before both their parents; to connect their hearts and to accept her new name.

The witnesses are there to agree with the two people that what they have vowed before God and man will be accomplished. One of the reasons I know most don't understand their purpose at the wedding is that when a divorce takes place, the witnesses who stood in agreement usually don't make a big deal about it!

These two people should have to repay them for all of the witnesses' expenses, since the wedding they agreed too was supposed to be forever. The audience seated on the right and left sides of the bride and groom is there for more than to bring gifts and attend the reception. They are held responsible as well to agree with the union, and to help it become what God intended it to be.

When used, lighting the unity candle indicates that a new person, with a new name and a new divine purpose, was just birthed in front of everyone in attendance. His father and mother and her father and mother aren't a part of this union, which is why their candles are blown out after lighting the one candle.

The receiving line at the reception is designed to recognize that this groom has found his good thing, the crown of his life and his virtuous woman, and to declare the beauty and elegance of his bride.

Jesus has given the church (Christians) a new name because we are betrothed to Him in marriage. Our old name is gone and everything about our relationship with Him puts Him first and the church (bride) second.

Do You Really Want to Get Married?

The time of total commitment begins once two people say, "I do," and become one.

Many women are more excited about the dress and the wedding ceremony than the actual marriage. Marriage is no joke, even though the movie industry does everything it can to make into a joke.

Living happily ever after is another movie theme that makes people feel all warm and fuzzy inside. But real life can take you far from feeling warm and fuzzy to trying to figure out what in the world you were thinking. It is then that a personal relationship with Christ, the third person in this union, becomes a must. It is also then that the mentors mentioned earlier and the spiritual leaders must shine a light on the situation. This is very seldom seen in the movies or on television.

The two people have become one in the marriage covenant, and their focus must be on the other person's needs even more than their own. The questions in Chapter 9 are designed to cause a person to think about the commitment marriage requires. Review the questions and answers there to determine if this is the right time for you to think about being married.

Marriage is one of the greatest institutions in the earth, but it will cost a person's life to make it work and to keep it advancing. Remove all of the Hollywood out of your mind concerning marriage so that you are ready to make a real marriage work.

A Godly Vision for Marriage

It is easy to think that God has changed His mind about marriage and its design, since man attempts to redefine the marital relationship. God's design, between a man and a woman only, works, since this is the only way that reproduction can take place. Remember, God told *them*, man and woman, to be fruitful and to replenish the earth.

There will always be attacks by the forces of hell against marriage, since everything on the earth proceeds and is given purpose from it. I believe the defense of marriage is not just holding rallies and forums to debate the issue (even though that is needed), but it is strengthening the marriages that exist between men and women in and outside of the church.

Teaching young people about what love really looks like so that lust can't masquerade as love will help to develop proper relationships. Giving a vision of an eternity with God where a human court doesn't rule will help many to make the right decision concerning their lives and conduct while living on the earth. Marriage is modeling the eternal marriage that can't be altered or misrepresented by anything man does on the earth.

Get ready to marry the true Groom and Keeper of your soul, and to become the true bride that has prepared herself through embracing grace and holiness.

AMEN!

Made in the USA
Lexington, KY
14 February 2015